STIRLING
IN COMBAT

*For my dear friend Christopher Shaw
(1964–90), a life so full of promise
cut tragically short.*

STIRLING
IN COMBAT

Jonathan Falconer
Foreword by Murray Peden

SUTTON PUBLISHING

First published in the United Kingdom in 1991 by
Ian Allan Ltd

This edition published in 2006 by
Sutton Publishing Limited · Phoenix Mill
Thrupp · Stroud · Gloucestershire · GL5 2BU

British Library Cataloguing in Publication Data
A catalogue record for this book is available from the British Library.

ISBN 0-7509-4114-6

Half title: Rivenhall, April 1945. No 570 Squadron's Stirling IV, LK292 W-Witch, with her groundcrew. *B. GIBBS*

Title Page: Rivenhall, March 1945. No 570 Squadron's Stirling IV, LK555 '555 State Express'. *J. STEWART*

Typeset in 10/15 pt Photina.
Typesetting and origination by
Sutton Publishing Limited.
Printed in Great Britain by
J. H. Haynes & Co. Ltd., Sparkford.

Contents

Following pilot training in his native Canada, Murray Peden came to England late in 1942 as a 19-year-old pilot officer to complete his training with Nos 12 OTU and 1651 HCU. He joined No 214 Squadron at Chedburgh in September 1943 as a pilot and flew a tour of operations on Stirlings and Fortresses. Awarded the DFC in September 1944, he was then posted to instruct with No 1699 CU until the war's end.

Peden followed a distinguished postwar career in Canada as a barrister and public servant. His appointments have included Crown Attorney, Province of Manitoba; Deputy Minister for Public Utilities; and Director of the Atlantic Council of Canada. Peden is author of *A Thousand Shall Fall*, the classic account of his wartime flying career with RAF Bomber Command.

Foreword

MURRAY PEDEN DFC, QC, BA, LLB

Vergil opens his great *Aeneid* with the evocative declaration: 'Of arms I sing and the hero, destiny's exile . . .'. With but slight change – for the Stirling was a heroine to Stirling aircrew – Jonathan Falconer could have used the same proud introduction for this eminently readable and well researched narrative of the Stirling at war. A heroine truly worthy of classical literature, the Stirling, too, can be viewed as destiny's exile. Pregnant with the capacity for greatness, she was doomed by short-sighted Air Ministry specifications, and, ironically, by the redemption of a much more serious failure, the Manchester, to be passed over for the renewed design effort which would have cured her one basic weakness, a lack-lustre altitude performance.

The Manchester's rebirth as the mighty Lancaster, under the inspired design ministrations of Roy Chadwick, put Sir Arthur Harris in possession of what he liked to call 'that Shining Sword', a superb weight-lifter and highly reliable performer. Not to have exploited that weapon would have been folly; even so, it was a questionable decision not to invest a little more effort in the Stirling, for she had displayed many solid attributes. Overall, she was a rugged, battle-worthy champion, not to be taken lightly.

Jonathan Falconer touches on one of her great accomplishments, a gift incidental to the yeoman service she did with Main Force, in citing the tremendous boost she gave civilian morale. In my view, the importance of that contribution simply cannot be over-estimated, bearing in mind that the new, awesomely proportioned bomber injected this powerful stimulus into British arteries at a time when such medication was sorely needed. In battle theatres scattered from Norway to North Africa, our Commonwealth armies had been hammered into a corner – where they had not been summarily ejected – awaiting further pounding from the seemingly invincible German forces.

Fighter Command's splendid battle in the skies over the Home Counties had given us at least one victory, putting the brake on the tidal wave of German success, but what is often overlooked is that victory was far from immediately apparent, and it was, despite its crucial importance, a purely defensive achievement. What the British people needed was what the Stirling soon provided: the sight of a fleet of bombers of majestic dimensions setting out from England's shores to 'give it back to them'. At the sound of those engines, people streamed into the streets to wave and shout exultant approval of their youthful emissaries roaring overhead outward bound on the nightly crusade. For Britons who were not eye witnesses, countless newspaper photographs of their mighty new weapon helped immeasurably to sustain a defiance and resolve long battered by the humiliating ascendancy of German arms.

Unfortunately, familiarity does have the effect popularly attributed to it, hence the evidence of that public support and satisfaction was not as frequently manifested by the time I appeared on the scene (September 1943) as a 19-year-old Stirling captain with No 214 Squadron. Nevertheless, every night, small groups of expectant admirers migrated to the boundaries of our drome at Chedburgh, as the twilight symphony of eighty Bristol Hercules engines, straining intermittently to full-throated bellowing on run-ups, foretold another behemoths' parade to the downwind end of the runway in use.

The ensuing scene is engraved on my mind. Unhurried as a chain of circus elephants, the ponderously-gaited Stirlings growled their way implacably around the perimeter track, making for the little caravan off the runway's end, where an Aldis lamp's green wink would launch each monster in turn on a thunderous search for flying speed. And if the sight of my helmeted head in that lofty canopy, trundling along with a bellyful of incendiaries and a couple of 2,000-pounders earmarked for a site in Germany, clearly gave those civilian witnesses deep satisfaction, the sight of their waves and thumbs-up exuberance helped steady my nerves too, as I sweated and braced myself for the strain of a war-load take-off in an aircraft that demanded meticulous handling during such exercises. Silent prayer was common, as well, on a muggy night and short runway.

In creating this book, the author has mined a broad vein of activities, and most dexterously selected events and information that capture the true flavour of many-faceted bomber operations. It is apparent that he harbours warm feelings for his subject. I have elsewhere recorded my own deep affection and respect for the remarkable qualities of the Stirling, so, lest in my approbation I be accused of inordinate bias, I point to the fact that at the beginning of 1944, after Stirlings had been taken off Main Force German targets, our No 214 Squadron aircrew were switched to the black Fortresses of No 100 Group, and thereafter despatched with Main Force to carry out radar-countermeasures operations. No one questions the fact that the B-17 was a superlative performer, an aircraft most unlikely to prompt her pilots to over-praise others.

I trust that this fine study by Jonathan Falconer will make it clear to readers that, far from discharging only a minor role, the Stirling was in fact Bomber Command's 'star turn' for some months, and followed that service with a lengthy period of extremely useful duty in a wide variety of supporting roles. The incidents Falconer has chronicled also tend to support the old maxim that Stirling crews frequently cited, to the effect that prospects of the violent corkscrew did not faze them, because 'the pilot will come apart before she will'. Understandably then, I still cherish a loyalty toward the old Stirling that only the highest merit could sustain.

On behalf of all Stirling aircrew, therefore, I bow to Patrick Henry and say defiantly: 'If this be bias . . . make the most of it.'

MURRAY PEDEN DFC, QC, BA, LLB
Winnipeg, Canada

Acknowledgements

In the preparation of this book, a great many people and organisations have given of their time, willingly and enthusiastically. Some of these people I have been fortunate enough to meet face to face; with others I have conducted lengthy correspondence, or discussed issues over the telephone, amassing a huge mountain of notes and correspondence in the process. Something that all these people share is a common interest in the Stirling and a desire to see it represented fairly in print after all these years.

A number of individuals who were involved with the Stirling during the Second World War deserve particular mention for their valuable contribution to this story of Shorts' big bomber: George McDowell (factory worker, Short Bros & Harland, Belfast), Alex Wood (pilot, XV Squadron), George Mackie (pilot, XV, 214, 46 Squadrons, 1651 HCU), A.T. Gamble (wireless operator, 620 Squadron), James McIlhinney (navigator, 218 Squadron), Lew Parsons (flight engineer, 75 (NZ) Squadron), Christ Dickenson (flight engineer, 75 (NZ) Squadron), Phil Dyson (pilot, 196 Squadron), Bob Grant (pilot, 218 Squadron), John MacFarland (navigator, 75 (NZ) Squadron), Ray Seeley (flight mechanic, 149 Squadron), Wally Legard (electrician, 1651 HCU), J. Hardman (fitter, 214 Squadron), Roy White (ordnance mechanic, Rivenhall), Frances I'Anson (factory worker, Sebro), Geoff Rothwell (pilot, 75, 218 and 138 Squadrons), Jack Grinham (wireless operator, SOE), John Hill (fitter, 6/8 MUs), John Hibbs (bomb aimer, 196 Squadron), Dixie Dean (Parachute Regiment) and Alistair McFarlane (historian).

Murray Peden, former Stirling pilot and the author of *A Thousand Shall Fall*, kindly agreed to write the Foreword.

Stirlings of No 299 Squadron at Keevil are marshalled ready to receive their cargoes of paratroopers for Phase II of Operation 'Tonga', 5 June 1944. *IWM CH21188*

John Reid, former photographic librarian of the Stirling Aircraft Society, has worked tirelessly and eagerly to provide an excellent selection of material from his archive; his contribution has been invaluable. Permission to reproduce these photographs is hereby acknowledged, with thanks.

John Chasemore, of the former Rover Group Ltd's Longbridge Photographic Department, deserves special thanks for tracking down the fine collection of photographs which depict Stirling production at the Austin Shadow Factories, and which are reproduced by kind permission of the British Motor Industry Heritage Trust.

Sarah Fraser and Derek Mercer assisted with the copying and printing of many of the photographs reproduced within.

Fellow author Ken Merrick 'down under' for help with tracking down and supplying photographs of SD Stirlings.

Photographs taken by the late Noel Chaffey are reproduced by kind permission of the Chaffey family.

Thanks are due also to Harper Collins Ltd for permission to quote from *The Sky Belongs to Them* by Dr Roland Winfield DFC, AFC (William Kimber, 1976).

I should also like to thank the following individuals and organisations for their valued contributions: Jack Atkins, Claude Backhouse, *Belfast Telegraph*, Jim Berry, BBC Radio Ulster, *Birmingham Evening Mail*, *Bristol Evening Post*, L. Brock, David Brook, Stan Brooks, George Blows, J. Brigden, *Cambridgeshire Evening News*, *Cambridgeshire Times*, Commonwealth War Graves Commission, Mrs Miriam Cohen, Jim Corry, 'Cherry' Cherrington, J. Earnshaw, Arthur Edgley, Ron Eeles, R. Elliot, *Basildon Evening Echo*, Martyn R. Ford-Jones, J.C. Garland, Stephen Grant, Norman Green, Norman Harrison, W. Harvey, Bill Higgs, John Hutchinson (Rolls-Royce plc), Imperial War Museum, Mrs D. Johnson, J. Klenk, *Liverpool Daily Post & Echo*, J.H. Llewellyn, *Manchester Evening News*, Mrs Madeleine Moulds, Ms Kate Mullan (Short Bros plc), *Newcastle Evening Chronicle*, R. Owers, Jack Parker, C.E. Proome, Public Record Office (The National Archives, Kew), Harry Rathban, Derek Reed, *Reading Evening Post*, Bruce Robertson, Bruce Stait, James Stewart, the *Yorkshire Evening Press*, J.D. Young.

And finally, my grateful thanks are due to Glad Stockdale and Bow Watkinson at Sutton Publishing for their important contributions to the design and image scanning for this book.

To everyone, a very big thank you.

Jonathan Falconer
Bradford-on-Avon, Wiltshire
January 2006

Introduction

Condemned and castigated by Air Ministry officials and 'Bomber' Harris alike for its inefficiency, the Stirling was the firstborn of the RAF's trio of four-engined heavy bombers, and the only one designed from the outset to take four engines.

If history with its flickering lamp looks unfavourably on the Stirling and its exaggerated shadow of disgrace, then it does so at its peril. Indeed, the Stirling had its share of development and operational problems, but many of these were inflicted upon it as the result of inexperience and political interference from a blinkered and vacillating Air Ministry – it was the first of an untried new breed and many of the prewar precepts which shaped its design rapidly became outmoded by the pressing demands of war.

Criticised for its inability to reach an acceptable operating altitude with a full bomb load, ridiculed for being unable to carry stores any larger than the 2,000lb armour-piercing bomb, and rumoured to be more than a handful to fly, the Stirling was introduced to the bombing role in February 1941 and finally withdrawn from Bomber Command's frontline force in November 1943 after suffering unacceptably high casualties during the hard-fought Battle of Berlin.

But what the critics both then and now have failed to grasp is that although the Stirling was a flawed weapon, it nevertheless offered the British public a strong and visible morale boost at a time when it was sorely needed. With memories of defeat at Dunkirk and the close-run Battle of Britain still fresh in the nation's mind, the bitterly cold winter of 1940/41 melted into spring and the evacuation of British troops from Greece. Rommel had the British 8th Army on the run in the North African Desert, while the Nazi U-boat packs lurking in the bitterly cold waters of the North Atlantic were tightening the noose on

Allied convoys as they stuck their necks out in a desperate bid to keep Britain supplied with vital war materials and foodstuffs.

With its broad, high shoulders and purposefully jutting chin, the Stirling bomber offered Churchill the teeth with which to give substance to the hitherto gummy image of the British bulldog. Whether or not it failed ultimately to live up to its tough image is largely immaterial; the fact remains that the Stirling was there at the right time to bolster the nation's spirits and to show that Britain could produce a bigger and stronger weapon than the enemy, capable of inflicting a deep and lasting wound.

On the operational side, the Stirling was generally loved by its crews for being tough, roomy and a joy to fly. With its rugged construction and near fighter manoeuvrability, it often proved more than a match for nightfighter adversaries and could soak up combat damage that would have downed a less robust aircraft. Stirlings of No 7 Squadron became the founding aircraft of the RAF's legendary Pathfinder Force in August 1942, and with the type's relegation to second, extended to cloak-and-dagger operations in the dead of night to support Resistance groups on the continent. Later versions of the Stirling carried paratroops and towed troop-carrying gliders into battle in support of such epic operations as 'Overlord', 'Market Garden' and 'Varsity' during the last two years of war, proving to all that the Stirling was still a valuable weapon in the RAF's inventory, and far from being a spent force. At the war's end, the Stirling squadrons helped in the repatriation of war-weary PoWs and political refugees from the maelstrom of postwar Europe, soldiering on in the transport role with the RAF at home and overseas until its ultimate withdrawal from service in 1946.

Stirling in Combat sets out to portray in words and pictures just what it was like to have been 'on Stirlings' during the Second World War. Drawing on personal recollections from a variety of sources, supported by other primary and secondary source material, the life of the Short Stirling is told in the words of those who knew it best – the men and women who built it and those who serviced and flew it in a variety of roles with the RAF.

The majority of the photographs in this book were previously unpublished when it first appeared in 1991, and vary widely in their quality. Official photographs taken with large-format plate cameras offer a technically finer image than the many taken surreptitiously by RAF personnel on treasured Box Brownies for their snapshot albums. In the case of the latter, black and white film was in very short supply during the war years and, in any case, photography without proper authorisation on RAF stations was strictly forbidden, for obvious reasons. But for those who wanted to record their wartime service in a few photographs, a friend in the station photographic section could often be bribed with a couple of pints of bitter and a packet of Passing Clouds to supply a few feet of safety film stock intended for aircraft cameras, cut down to fit the much narrower film size of the Brownie.

The Bristol Hercules engine was used to good effect in the Stirling – as this advertisement for the Bristol company emphasises.

The Stirling was conceived as a result of the RAF's prewar expansion scheme. Short Brothers of Rochester tendered successfully for two prototype high-speed, long-range, four-engined strategic bombers, to be built to Specification B12/36 which had been issued in July 1936. Soon afterwards, an initial production order was placed for 200 'straight off the drawing board'.

A crew of six would be carried, and armament was to comprise power-operated multi-gun turrets in the nose and tail, together with a ventral turret to protect against attacks from below. The largest stores to be carried by the new bomber were the 2,000lb AP and/or standard 500lb bombs. Normal all-up weight was to be 48,000lb.

In its specification, the Air Ministry decreed that the wing span should not exceed 100ft in order to conform with existing hangar dimensions. This was to become a serious handicap for the Stirling in its operational career because the low-aspect ratio wing created severe altitude limitations.

Below: Shorts chose to build a half-scale prototype during 1939, known as the S31/M4, which first flew from Rochester amid great secrecy on 19 September 1938. At the controls was Shorts' Chief Test Pilot, John Lankester Parker, accompanied by a Shorts employee called Hugh Gordon. Concern was expressed over the prototype's excessively long take-off and landing runs. To rectify this problem, wing incidence was increased from 3½° to 6½°.

However, tooling-up at Shorts' Rochester factory had reached an advanced stage so it was too late to effect a modification. Instead a compromise was reached. The undercarriage was lengthened to increase the angle of attack, retracting in two stages: vertically, then backwards into the nacelle. This modification was incorporated satisfactorily into the S31, although its mainwheels retracted with a single movement only.

Above: The first of two full-size prototypes, L7600 took to the air on 14 May 1939 but, on landing back at Rochester, one of its wheel brakes seized, collapsing the stalky undercarriage. The aircraft bellied-in and was written off – a major setback to the Stirling programme. *IWM MH5155*

Next spread: A redesigned and strengthened undercarriage was fitted to the second prototype, L7605, which first flew on 3 December with the undercarriage locked down, just in case. A second flight was made on 24 December when the undercarriage was successfully retracted and lowered, whereafter the flight test programme proceeded on schedule. The first production aircraft took to the air five months later on 7 May 1940. *AUTHOR*

In choosing photographs for inclusion in this book, the main criterion has been to rate interest value of the subject above technical quality of the image. Where the official pictures win on technical prowess, the unofficial ones stand head and shoulders above them in their strong evocation of time and place, pathos and elation; snapshots they are in many instances, recording a short glimmer in time of a brief life, soon to be snuffed out for ever in the dark night skies over Germany.

Stirling in Combat is not intended to be the final and definitive work on the subject, but rather an impression of the Stirling and of the many people who were involved in its service with the RAF throughout the greater part of the Second World War.

A Giant
is Born

With the swirling storm clouds of war already gathering as the earnest little figure of Neville Chamberlain stepped from his aircraft at Heston in September 1938, declaring 'peace for our time', the Ministry of Aircraft Production's (MAP) Scheme 'L' adopted in April was well under way. Its self-delusory aim was to boost the RAF's inventory of frontline fighters and bombers to a strength of 1,352 bombers and 608 fighters by April 1940, yet in September 1939 the RAF would enter war with 608 fighters – but only 536 bombers.

An initial production order for 100 Stirlings was placed with Short Brothers at Rochester in 1939, followed by a further order of 100 placed with Short Bros & Harland at its new factory in Belfast, Northern Ireland. With the worsening of international relations in Europe, Stirling production orders at Rochester and Belfast were soon extended to 1,500 aircraft. New contracts were also placed with Austin Motors at its huge Longbridge factory in Birmingham and, before long, Stirling components were being built in some twenty factories centred around Rochester, the West and South Midlands, and across the Irish Sea in Belfast.

The Stirling's modular construction lent itself to dispersed production techniques, but strict supervision was needed to maintain standards. Shorts and the MAP assembled a mobile group of 600 production engineers and draughtsmen whose job it was to visit the dispersed factories in England and Northern Ireland to co-ordinate production of the bomber.

In Northern Ireland, Short Bros & Harland's main Stirling factory was located at Queen's Island, with the adjacent airport at Sydenham used for test-flying. Before long, Stirlings were also assembled and test-flown at Aldergrove, Long Kesh and Maghaberry. Production began at Queen's Island in June 1940.

Assembly of the all-metal fuselage sections was accomplished with the use of large vertical wooden jigs. Here, the rear fuselage section takes shape at Austin Motors' Longbridge factory in the West Midlands. In the background can be seen the front centre fuselage section containing the wing spar frames. An unusual feature was the continuation of the top wing covering across the inside of the fuselage, with a large circular hole cut in the centre for access to oxygen bottles stowed above. *BRISTOL MOTOR INDUSTRY HERITAGE TRUST (BMIHT)*

A major production line for the Stirling was established at Austin Motors' factory at Longbridge, Birmingham, and was supplied with components and sub-assemblies from a number of surrounding shadow factories. The main subsections (ie, fuselage and wings) were built at Longbridge then transported across the city by low-loader to the shadow factory at Bickenhill Lane, Marston Green. Here, assembly was completed, engines installed and propellers fitted. Engines were then ground-run for tuning and synchronisation, and the aircraft towed out of the back gate to Elmdon Airport for initial flight tests in readiness for collection by ATA pilots and eventual delivery to the RAF.

The tail section of Austin-built Mk III EH879, minus fin and horizontal stabilisers, is well on the way to completion during March 1943. Next it will be mated with the three other independently assembled sections that make up the Stirling's fuselage, before its Frazer-Nash FN20A tail turret is installed. In addition to the bolting together of the frames, lap plates were riveted to the exterior of each joint. *BMIHT*

'In My Beginning is My End': Longbridge, mid-1943. As if to emphasise the short life expectancy of a heavy bomber and its crew, within months of this photograph being taken, the two aircraft nearest the camera were lost on operations. Mk III EH883 passed to No 149 Squadron on 20 May and failed to return from Mannheim on 23/24 September, while EH884 joined No 218 Squadron on 18 May, only to be lost on ops to Turin on 16/17 August. *BMIHT*

Riveter and 'Dolly' girl (one who holds a rivet block on the inside of the structure to enable the riveter to work from the outside, fixing light alloy sheets to the frame) at work on the outer engine nacelle. Spring clips were used to hold the metal skin in place before riveting. Female labour was employed extensively in factories of the Stirling group. *BMIHT*

However, initial production was lamentably slow, due mainly to delays in tooling up, compounded by a switch in priority from four to twin and single-engined aircraft to meet the losses sustained by the RAF in the Battle of Britain, raging in the skies of southern England at that time. Uninvited visits by the Luftwaffe to Queen's Island on 14 August 1940, and Rochester on 15 August, resulted in the destruction on the ground of 11 semi-completed airframes and quantities of stored components.

Following the bombing of Shorts' Rochester factory, its vulnerability to air attack was realised and the need for dispersed production appreciated.

Consequently, a major production line for Stirlings was established at South Marston near Swindon, with shadow factories close by at Blunsdon and Highworth, and at the Gloster Works at Hucclecote near Gloucester. Shorts also established a drawing office at Stratton St Margaret near Swindon.

Above: Like the fuselage, the mainplane was an all-metal structure, built around two spars, covered with light alloy sheet and flush-riveted. Here, finishing touches are made to the starboard wing although it has yet to be fitted with fuel and oil tanks, Gouge flaps, bomb cells, engines and undercarriage.

In accordance with the colour-coding of pipework introduced on British military aircraft in 1916, and further extended by the RAF in the Second World War, the various systems were identified by colour-coded bands at intervals along the piping: black for oil, red for fuel, white for hydraulic, blue for coolant, etc.

An array of control rods, hoses, pipes and wires can be seen, some bundled loosely together, for eventual connection of their life-giving controls once the wing has been attached to the fuselage. *BMIHT*

Next spread: Calling all Workers: a busy scene at Austin's Longbridge factory early in 1941, as a Stirling Mk I Srs I takes shape. *BMIHT*

William Harvey lived in Belfast during the early years of the war and went to work in one of the many factories – large and small – which had been turned over to war production. Originally, Mackies' was a large textile engineering foundry before it became a part of the Stirling's dispersed production programme.

A Stirling Mk I Srs I of the first batch to be built at Short Bros & Harland's Belfast factory during the summer of 1940. In the foreground can be seen wing sections and undercarriage nacelle fairings for Handley Page Herefords which, at that time, were being built under licence from their parent company. *SHORTS*

In 1940, I started work as an apprentice fitter in Mackies' aircraft factory, Belfast, where the tailplane, control column and undercarriage for the Stirling were built. These components were transported to the main factory of Shorts' at Sydenham for final assembly.

My last job at Mackies' was setting up part of the undercarriage known as the drag member. This was the part that came down from the back and joined the main struts; when the undercarriage was retracted it dragged the whole lot back inside the nacelle.

The jig for the drag member was built behind a large vertical machine which was operated by a girl who worked at other jobs while I was

The Stirling was broken down into several main assemblies to facilitate dispered production at a number of shadow factories and sub-contractors across the British Isles. The semi-complete wings and fuselage were transported by Ministry of Aircraft Production (MAP) low-loaders to final assembly points at such locations as Rochester Airport, Marston Green, South Marston or Sydenham.

On occasions, to suit production requirements, Stirling fuselage sections were shipped from Stranraer on the UK mainland to Larne in Northern Ireland for completion in Belfast. One of the first of these loads lost its DF loop, radio aerial and mid-upper turret under the stone arches that span the Larne-Carrickfergus-Belfast road at Magheramorne. Thereafter, these components were sent over packed safely inside the fuselage. Even so, MAP low-loaders often had to be dragged under the arches with tyres deflated to allow safe passage. Note the 'Monica' aerial beneath the rear turret of this Austin-built Mk III, LK593, en route to Marston Green early in 1944. *BMIHT*

setting up. The two main struts were made from steel and the cross-piece at the top was made from a light alloy.

When these were put in place there were still a lot of distance pieces to be fitted in, and these were all clamped. When it was ready for drilling, the girl swung the head of the machine round to the jig and drilled.

All the parts were then removed and taken to the work benches where they were deburred and then bolted together. I then put the whole lot, as one member, back into the jig to make sure that it was all right and there was no spring in the struts, before it was inspected by the AID [Aeronautical Inspection Directorate]. It was then built into a complete undercarriage and tested as if it was actually in the aircraft.

George McDowell was 17 years old when he left his job as an apprentice in a Belfast foundry and joined Shorts' at Queen's Island. Initially, he worked on the Handley Page Hereford and Bristol Bombay, both of which were being built under contract from their respective manufacturers. But in 1940 he was transferred to work on the giant Stirling.

George McDowell of Short Bros & Harland in Belfast, pictured in 1944. *G. McDOWELL*

Opposite: Semi-completed Mk III fuselages on the Longbridge production line in March 1943 await transport to Marston Green for final assembly. BK818 in the immediate foreground joined No XV Squadron in May, passing to No 1661 HCU at the end of 1943 and survived the war, only to be struck off charge (SOC) on 18 May 1945. *BMIHT*

I was transferred to the engine installation department for the Stirling at Queen's Island, known to us as Centre 75. All the different departments were called centres, each with a different number.

The engines were brought into the shop and put on a jig with four wheels. Oil coolers were fitted along with parts to the reduction gear box. The shaft of the engine was turned by hand so that the master spline was kept at the top of the engine, facilitating the fitting of the propeller which came in kit form and was assembled and tested before installation. The engines were then pushed out to their allotted positions in front of the aircraft before being attached to the wings.

In Centre 75 there were about thirty riggers who made all the control cables which, when completed, were taken to the test house for proof-loading. Oil tanks were also installed and fitted in the nacelles by this centre.

I was put to work along with a chap called Billy Clarke who had already been working on the Exactor controls. We fitted pipes from the fuselage through to the throttle box, and when the wings were joined to the fuselage we connected the pipes together at the wing root. These were easily identified by the colour of the identification tape on each system: oil, de-icing, fuel, etc. The pipes were ⅜th-inch copper and joined together by 'Ermeto' couplings.

Before the Exactor oil was put into the system, it had to be air-tested. The pipes in the nacelle to the Exactor were blanked off along with the

pipe to the CSU (Constant Speed Unit), situated on the engine casing behind the propellers and forward of the cylinders. I disconnected all the pipes at the throttle box and, with the piece of test equipment I had made, all these pipes were joined together, allowing the whole system to be air-tested in one operation.

A high-pressure air cylinder with a gauge was connected to the pipes at the CSU and opened up with a bottle key. When the pressure went up to 1,000lb/sq in it was shut off. If the pressure stayed at 1,000lb/sq in for 20 minutes, the system was all right. But if it dropped, I went around all the connections with a milk bottle filled with soapy water and a little paint brush until I had found the leak.

If the system held, I called the Works Inspector who waited for
20 minutes to see the air blown through all the pipes in order to show
that the complete system was being tested. The test gear was removed at
the throttle box and all pipes reconnected to all the reservoirs. Exactor oil
(paraffin) was then put into each reservoir and pumped to each Exactor
in the nacelle, and to the CSU. The system was then primed.

Control rods were now connected to the engines in the nacelles which
meant that the throttle levers in the throttle box were operating to the
carburettor. What was then required was to set the throttles, getting the
same travel, keeping the levers all in line and getting the same readings
(degrees) at SLOW RUN, CRUISING, RATED and TAKE-OFF. This part of the
job is quite complicated to explain as there was no set pattern to achieve
the desired outcome. The two mixture levers (which were for fuel

economy) only worked when the throttle levers were in the CRUISING position. The four levers on the throttle box for airscrew control operated the CSU, which in turn operated the pitch, or feathering, of the propeller blades. The automatic pilot or 'Iron Man' was also assembled in Centre 75. (The Exactor controls were eventually done away with. A new system was put in its place, called Mech Eng Controls, consisting of tie-rods, cables, pulleys and cable drums.)

The wheel-braking system, air bottles and piping to the undercarriage wheels were also tested, together with the aircraft's oxygen and boost systems.

A fuel flow test was also made. This test required the use of a very clean drum, calibrated on the inside. The operator had control of the fuel by operating a valve on a flexible pipe. When the pipe was switched on, the valve was opened and the fuel flowed into the drum. A Works Inspector and an AID official had a stop watch and timed the flow into the drum. When this test was being done the Fire Service was always standing-by and the hangar doors kept open since the fuel was 100 Octane.

Finally, the cylinders were inhibited and then the sparking plugs were greased and fitted. The aircraft was now almost ready for ground running and engine synchronisation.

In 1937, at the age of 15, Jim Corry started work at the Rover car factory, Acocks Green, Birmingham, close to where he lived. In 1940, like many 'Brummies', he became involved in the Stirling production programme centred around the enormous Austin Shadow Factory at Longbridge.

In 1940 I was transferred from Rover Aero Factory No 1 at Acocks Green to the X-ray Department at Rover Aero Factory No 2, Solihull. It was there that I became involved in X-raying components for the four-engined Stirling bomber. We worked shifts as

Left: Queen's Island, Belfast, January 1944: newly assembled Stirlings await ground running and engine synchronisation before flight-testing at nearby Sydenham. Dominating the foreground is a pristine Mk III, EF310, which went on to serve with No 1654 HCU before being SOC on 28 March 1946. In the background can be seen several examples of the Stirling's stablemate, the Sunderland flying boat, with which it shared many design features. *SHORTS*

Next spread: Last Stirling in the shop: the last Stirling to be delivered from Austin's in late 1944, pictured with its workforce at Elmdon. LK619 bears an emblem on her nose depicting a scantily-clad female sitting on the edge of a bath, with the legend 'The Last Dip in Golden Fleece' beneath. *BMIHT*

Above: The end of the beginning: somewhere in England, mid-1943. Flt Capt Joan Hughes MBE, Air Transport Auxiliary, signs the delivery note for an anonymous Stirling III before flying it to a frontline squadron or maintenance unit, opening another chapter in the aircraft's uncertain future.

With the level of attrition suffered by the type at this point of the war, it could well have become a casualty within days of joining a squadron. This photograph gives some impression of the lofty position and good visibility enjoyed from the Stirling's cockpit, some 22ft above the ground.

Left: Belfast-built Stirling IIIs are test-flown from Sydenham in the late spring of 1943 to check for any snags before delivery to the RAF by No 8 Ferry Pilots' Pool. *SHORTS*

we were very busy and needed to have these parts X-rayed for despatch to other shadow factories, mainly to Austin's at Longbridge.

If I ever was to become an aircrew member I didn't want to go in a Stirling because I knew the X-raying of components was very random. For instance, we checked twelve cylinder sleeves in crates and picked one at random for a full X-ray. The other eleven just had a small head part X-rayed. However, in 1942 I joined the Royal Navy, so that was that with me for Stirlings!

Madeleine Moulds lived close to the Marson Green Shadow Factory where she worked in the offices of the Inspection Department.

When the first Longbridge-built Stirling was taking its test-flight, there were many anxious faces in the Inspection Department; there were always snags galore.

One day, one of these huge aircraft was standing outside waiting for faults to be put right. I walked underneath as I often did on an errand. A short time afterwards, the undercarriage collapsed and the whole machine was flat on the floor. I don't think I ever walked or stood under another!

View from the Cockpit

Despite its inability to carry a heavy bomb load at high altitude over a long distance, the Stirling was a joy to fly, although its vices on take-off and landing needed to be respected and mastered. Crouching on the ground, its spindly undercarriage and jutting chin made it look ungainly, but once airborne it was in its true element and assumed the grace and agility of a huge dragonfly.

Alex Wood was a Stirling pilot with No XV Squadron at Mildenhall. His seventeenth op on 3 October 1943 to Kassel proved to be his last when his

On first impression to the crews joining heavy conversion units from OTUs, the Stirling was a monster because of its sheer size and, in particular, its height from the ground. Most OTUs were equipped with the Vickers Wellington, which was, by comparison, quite a stubby aircraft. *BMIHT*

Stirling III, BF470:G, was shot down by a nightfighter from 3/NJG1 near Osnabrück. Wood's flight engineer was killed in the hail of cannon shells from the fighter, but the rear gunner managed to bag the attacker – a Ju88. The damage to G-George was so severe that Wood ordered the crew to bale out. His two gunners never jumped and perished in the crash, but Wood and the surviving three crew members lived to sit out the rest of the war in captivity at Stalag IVB.

Of all the heavy bombers of the Second World War the Short Stirling was, without doubt, the roomiest and most comfortable for all the crew. It was a tragedy that its usefulness was reduced so much as the result of shortening its wing-span from the original design.

Above: As a result of the high wing-loadings caused by the shortening of its wingspan, the Stirling had a high rate of roll and was so manoeuvrable that it could turn inside most Second World War fighters, except the Hawker Hurricane.

This Stirling I, pictured in the late summer of 1942, bears the likeness of Jimminy Cricket, Pinocchio's 'conscience', on its nose. *IWM CH6365*

Opposite: The Office: Pilot, second pilot and bomb aimer in the cockpit of an early Stirling I of No 7 Squadron during 1941. *AUTHOR*

My introduction to the Stirling was with the Mk I at the beginning of 1943 when I was posted to No 1657 HCU at Stradishall. The first two weeks were spent in the classroom learning all about the systems of the aircraft and in the Link Trainer. On my first flight, my initial impression was of the height above the ground of the pilot, and at first there was a tendency to either fly into the ground upon landing, or to over-compensate and flare out too high. This soon passed, however, and I

became able to judge height above the ground accurately and effect mostly good landings.

During the two weeks of conversion flying there was a consistently moderate wind of about strength five, almost exactly halfway between the two main runways, so there was always a crosswind. It was necessary, therefore, to learn quickly how to correct and anticipate the strong tendency of the aircraft to swing on take-off and landing – of which more in a moment.

First pilot's seat and instrument panel in a Stirling.

IWM E (MOS) 648

Due to the very high winding-loading which resulted from the shortening of the wing-span, the stalling speed – and consequently the take-off and landing speeds – was very high for those days. The stalling speed with wheels and flaps down was 110mph (theoretically 107mph with a clean new aircraft), take-off speed 125–135mph, depending on the loaded weight, approach speed 125mph, and touchdown 110mph.

Once airborne, with wheels and flaps up, the Stirling came to life. It was light and responsive on the controls and I considered it to be a very safe aircraft with few vices. It required very little rudder in turns and was so manoeuvrable that it could turn inside most Second World War fighters, except the Hurricane.

The stall was gentle and predictable and the aircraft did not drop a wing. Asymmetric flight with one engine feathered was not difficult because the rudder load could be trimmed out.

I recall a discussion one morning – prompted by the tendency of the Halifax Mk I to spin uncontrollably – between pilots of 'B' Flight, as to whether the Stirling could be made to spin and, if so, if it could recover. The outcome was that we spent about two hours trying all we knew to induce a spin, but without success. The best we could do was a steep spiral.

On and near the ground, however, the Stirling had a number of vices, some serious and others merely annoying. Its tendency to swing on take-off resulted from the almost total blanketing of the fin and rudder by the fuselage during the transitional period between the tailwheels leaving the ground and the tail-up position on take-off. This was equally so on touchdown until the tailwheels settled on landing, causing the aircraft to act as a weather vane and swing into wind. Whilst I was stationed at Stradishall, some ten aircraft were written off or badly damaged on the aerodrome as the result of swings which got out of control on take-off or landing, due to persistent crosswinds, causing the tall undercarriage to collapse.

To avoid serious swing it was necessary to anticipate the direction of swing, opening the appropriate throttles to correct it. There was always a swing to the right due to the torque effect of all propellers rotating in the same direction (anti-clockwise). So, the starboard throttles were invariably opened fully and the port throttles partially, until full rudder control was obtained with the tail fully raised at about 60mph.

An annoying and uncomfortable vice – especially for the rear gunner – although it was not hazardous, was the tendency of the tailwheels to shimmy if the aircraft was three-pointed on landing. To avoid this uncomfortable trait, which threw the rear gunner about in his turret and continued until the aircraft had stopped at the end of the landing run, it was first necessary to land on the main wheels only. Then, with the tailwheels as close to the ground as possible, they would drop almost immediately to give steerage and thus reduce the tendency to swing.

On posting to No XV Squadron at Mildenhall in August 1943, the most noticeable difference from the pilot's viewpoint was the change from Exactor throttle controls of the Mk I to cable controls of the Mk III, which made a vast improvement. It gave much finer adjustment: the old system needed to be primed every 20 minutes by opening fully each throttle in turn.

Flying performance seemed to vary greatly from one aircraft to another. For example, my machine would climb to over 18,000ft fully laden on the approach to a target, whereas other pilots said they had difficulty in reaching 15,000ft with their aircraft. I found that a cruising speed of 230mph, while using slightly more fuel, was overall more economical because the increased speed gave an aerodynamically cleaner aircraft without the familiar nose-up attitude. That same speed was even more economical homeward bound over the North Sea when the boost could be reduced, with a very gradual loss of altitude at the rate of less than 100ft/min.

I consistently produced better than average fuel consumption figures, as well as having the altitude-over-target record for the squadron at 18,500ft. My bombing run was then carried out in a shallow dive to spend as little time as possible over the heavily defended area. The only exception to that method was when attacking Berlin where the defended area was so large as to render it impracticable.

Thus, in the hands of an experienced pilot, the Stirling could climb to some 18,000ft, a respectable height for a fully laden four-engined heavy bomber during the Second World War, dispelling the myths that it was underpowered and incapable of operating above 11,000ft. However, the majority of Stirling pilots were inexperienced, unwitting victims of the production-line training scheme to churn out new bomber crews. The HCUs simply did not have the time or resources to fine-tune the flying skills of every pilot who passed through their hands.

Because many newly qualified Stirling pilots had insufficient experience on the type, they could not hope immediately to master the idiosyncrasies of its handling characteristics; and because they could not get the best out of the big bomber from the outset, the odds against survival began to stack up against them.

'Men Who Go Up in the Air'

T he early Stirlings carried a crew of seven, comprising first and second pilot, navigator (who was also the bomb aimer), front gunner (who was also the wireless operator), two air gunners, and a flight engineer, who manned a gun if required. By the end of 1942, the crew position of second pilot had been abolished and a dedicated bomb aimer added to the crew.

With the change of role forced upon the Stirling in early 1944, the crew of a Special Duties or paratroop/glider-tug Stirling comprised pilot, navigator, bomb

Meet the Gang: A smiling Plt Off Derek de Rome RAAF poses for the camera beside Stirling IV LJ566 'Yorkshire Rose II', with his No 620 Squadron crew at Fairford in mid-1944. From left to right, back to front: Flt Sgt Brian Garwood, bomb aimer; Plt Off Ben Crocker, navigator; Flt Sgt Frank Pearman, flight engineer; Plt Off Derek de Rome, pilot; WO Noel Chaffey, wireless operator; Flt Sgt Pete Griffin, rear gunner. *N. CHAFFEY*

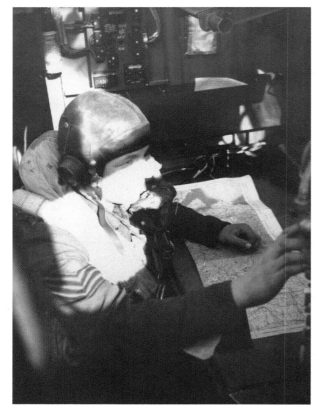

Above, left: Pilot: Plt Off Derek de Rome sits at the controls of a No 620 Squadron Stirling IV. On the early production Stirlings many pilots found difficulty in reaching the rudder bar with their feet, even with the cumbersome and heavy seat fully forward. *N. CHAFFEY*

Above, right: Bomb Aimer: Flt Sgt Brian Garwood is pictured in the bomb aimer's position down in the nose of Stirling IV LJ566. He is using a course-setting bomb sight, probably a Mk IX. *N. CHAFFEY*

Left: Navigator: seated at his station on the port side of the cockpit coupe facing outwards, the navigator occupied a position below and behind the pilot, with a blackout curtain to separate him from the flightdeck. At the after end of the coupe, an armour-plated bulkhead with sliding door gave access to the flight engineer and wireless operator's stations in the fuselage centre section, forward of the main spar.

On the chart table can be seen a 1:250,000 scale topographical map used by navigators for air map reading over strategically important regions of the Continent, particularly the industrial centres. *N. CHAFFEY*

Flight Engineer (Lofty Matthews, KIA Arnhem 1944) and Wireless Operator (John Wary, who survived the war): Flt Sgt Keith Prowd RAAF's No 196 Squadron crew flew Stirling IVs from Keevil during the spring and summer of 1944. Prowd's engineer and wireless op are seen here at their stations, located aft of the flight compartment and just forward of the main spar, in their Stirling IV. *K. PROWD via K.A. MERRICK*

Mid-Upper Gunner: Designed as a replacement for the early conical Frazer-Nash FN7, the FN50 mid-upper turret was fitted to late Stirling Is and IIIs. The FN7 had been unpopular with gunners due to its cramped interior and the difficulty it posed should an emergency escape need to be made. The rear doors of the turret had been sealed after a number of fatal accidents involving gunners who had struck the tailplane after bailing out. Thereafter, escape exits from the fuselage were used instead. Jack Pollack is pictured in the mid-upper turret of Stirling III EE963:N of No 149 Squadron during August 1943.
D. ODDY via JOHN REID/ STIRLING BOMBER RESEARCH LIBRARY *(JR/SBRL)*

Rear Gunner: Sgt Ted Harris of No 199 Squadron grins for the camera, ensconced in his FN20 turret with clear-vision panel removed. North Creake, 1944.

C. MUNRO via JR/SBRL

aimer/map reader, wireless operator/despatcher, rear gunner and flight engineer.

The Stirlings of No 199 (SD) Squadron, which flew radio countermeasures operations in 1944–5, carried a crew of eight which comprised pilot, navigator, flight engineer, wireless operator, three gunners and a special operator for the Mandrel jamming equipment carried.

Battle is Joined

Against the vapour-trailed backdrop of the Battle of Britain raging in the summer skies over England, the first production Stirling I was delivered to No 7 Squadron at Leeming Bar in Yorkshire on Friday 12 August 1940. Operational testing of the new aircraft had been assigned to the squadron under the command of Wg Cdr Paul Harris, a veteran of the Battle of Heligoland Bight in December the previous year.

From the outset, the Stirling fell prey to a number of difficult teething problems, the most serious of which involved the Exactor throttles. Because of the Stirling's size, a decision had been taken to replace traditional throttle and pitch control runs with Exactor controls. Levers in the cockpit were pushed, causing small pistons to compress oil in the pipelines leading to the engines, where the oil pressure moved another set of pistons which moved an actuating arm. In principle, the system was a good idea, requiring less force to operate than the traditional mechanically-actuated controls.

In practice it could prove potentially dangerous to the unwary. Because the Exactor system was unpressurised, it suffered from a time-lag, and many take-off swings for which the Stirling became renowned were as a result of throttle-lag. Exactors also had the tendency of resetting themselves, altering control settings, so pilots were constantly busy trying to synchronise the engines. At altitude they were also prone to freezing up.

A cause of almost equal concern was the Stirling's tall, stalky undercarriage and its feeble electric retraction motors which were prone to burning out under the strain. In the coming months, the electrical systems of the Stirling would be the cause of much frustration, giving rise to a report from Air Vice-Marshal Arthur Harris (then Deputy Chief of the Air Staff) to the Chief of the Air Staff,

On 12 August 1940, N3641 became the first Stirling to join No 7 Squadron, and by September the squadron had four on strength. However, the type was plagued with so many snags that it was declared unfit for operations until the problems had been resolved.

On 20 November 1940, Air Vice-Marshal Bob Saundby, Senior Air Staff Officer at Bomber Command, wrote to the Under Secretary of State for Air: 'I do not consider that the use of these valuable aircraft on operations over enemy territory will be justified until the operating height can be increased . . . to a minimum of 15,000ft.'

The first production Stirling I Srs Is were fitted with underpowered Hercules II radial engines and equipped with Frazer-Nash FN5A nose, FN25A ventral and FN4A tail turrets, armed with 0.303in machine guns. Mk I Srs I aircraft did away with the retractable ventral turret which had shown a tendency to extend itself on taxying, through vibration, replacing it with a provision for two beam-mounted FN55A 0.303in machine guns in the fuselage sides. The rear turret was also replaced in due course with the improved FN20A.

The Stirling's defensive armament was established from the 81st aircraft off the production line, in the guise of the Srs III. Armament was augmented with the addition of a Frazer-Nash FN7A dorsal turret armed with two 0.303in machine guns. The Mk I Srs III aircraft were also re-engined with the more powerful 1,500hp Hercules XI engines, equipped with two-speed superchargers. *IWM CH3137*

The Stirling suffered with troublesome undercarriage retraction motors which proved inadequate for the heavyweight tasks they were called upon to undertake. If this was not enough, the tall undercarriage was prone to collapse with the force of side-loadings during take-off or landing. The vulnerable joint is painted white in this photograph of N3641's undercarriage.

The largest British tyre on an operational aircraft during the Second World War was the main landing wheel of the Stirling. Manufactured by Dunlop, the whole wheel weighed 764lb, and measured 72½in in diameter and 28¾in in width. G. BLOWS

Marshal of the RAF Sir Charles Portal, on 26 April 1941 in which he summed up the problems. The electrical equipment in the Stirling, he opined, should have been a power engineering job, and that only a complete redesign of the electrical system could hope to solve the problems.

Until these problems could be rectified, the Stirling was relegated to non-operational status as a trainer. This enforced sidelining was used to good effect by the air and groundcrews to familiarise themselves with their new charges. No 7 Squadron moved to Oakington on 29 October 1940, where it would remain for the rest of the war. By January 1941, the squadron had seven Stirling Is on strength.

Evidence of the problems with the Stirling's undercarriage can be seen in the background of this photograph of No 7 Squadron Stirling Is at Oakington. *IWM CH5289*

Despite the continuing technical problems, pressure during early 1941 from Winston Churchill, the Prime Minister, and Lord Beaverbrook, Minister for Aircraft Production, resulted in the Stirling's first operational sortie in the late evening of 10 February when three aircraft, supported by fourteen Wellingtons, bombed oil storage tanks. All three Stirlings returned safely to Oakington.

Piecemeal operational sorties continued throughout the spring, hampered by recurrent technical problems and bad weather, but thankfully without loss. Then Bomber Command lost its first Stirling to the enemy on 9/10 April. A deep penetration raid to Berlin – 'the Big City' – had been ordered, although none of the three No 7 Squadron crews which operated that night got anywhere near their target. N6011, skippered by Flt Lt V. Pike, was shot down over western Germany near Lingen by a Messerschmitt Bf110 of 7/NJG1.

During April, a second Stirling squadron was formed at Wyton. Under the command of Wg Cdr H.R. Dale, No XV Squadron flew its first op to Berlin on 30 April. However, Dale was not to last for very long as the squadron's CO: he was shot down in Stirling I N3654, over western Holland in the early hours of 11 May, by a Bf110 of 4/NJG1 and died with all his crew.

By the end of June 1942, the RAF had accepted about fifty Stirlings; both Stirling squadrons had lost three aircraft each on operations, while No 7 Squadron had lost a further four in accidents.

The first Austin-built Stirling, W7426, is prepared for a flight test from Elmdon in July 1941. *BMIHT*

No 7 Squadron's Stirling I
N3641 was one of three
Stirlings that flew the type's
first offensive operation of
the war to Rotterdam on
10 February 1941.
IWM E (MOS) 674

The month of July saw the Stirling's first brief introduction to daylight raids on what were known as 'circus' operations. Small formations of bombers, escorted by a strong fighter force, would attack targets in France and the Low Countries in the hope of luring enemy fighters up so they could be picked off by the escorting Spitfires and Hurricanes.

Between July and December, Bomber Command was involved in a number of sorties to the French port of Brest where the German battlecruisers *Scharnhorst*, *Gneisenau* and *Prinz Eugen* were holed up. Stirlings were among the attacking forces on these occasions and scored a hit on the *Scharnhorst* on 23 July after it had moved south to La Pallice.

Meanwhile, the Stirling's involvement in the growing night offensive continued, with attacks on targets in Germany, while the first truly long-range sortie by the type was carried out on 10/11 September when both squadrons sent a combined force of 13 aircraft to bomb Turin in Italy, without loss.

With the U-boat war in the Atlantic going badly for the Allies, Bomber Command's attention was further divided in attacks on the yards building

On the night of 17/18 March 1941, Bomber Command despatched a mixed force of fifty-seven bombers, including one Stirling, to attack Bremen in support of the Allied campaign against the Nazi U-boat construction yards and bases. This was the first time that a Stirling had raided a target in Germany. The token aircraft, N3652, was supplied by No 7 Squadron and piloted by its 'B' Flight Commander Sqn Ldr P. Lynch-Blosse, carrying a 9,000lb bomb load. No aircraft were lost on this raid.

The PR photograph taken on the day after the raid shows:

1. A small hole in the roof of a covered slipway.
2. A possible crater close to an air raid shelter constructed on a cleared site.
3. Two submarines under new types of covered shelters; a third is in the south floating dock.
4. The cruiser *Seydlitz* and three destroyers fitting out at berths. *B. ROBERTSON*

No XV Squadron became the second squadron to equip with Stirlings when it re-formed at Wyton in April 1941. *IWM CH3296*

U-boats on the Baltic and North Sea coasts of Germany. In fact, the year 1941 acted as a prelude to greater involvement by the Stirling in a variety of bombing operations the following year. Valuable experience had been gained in bombing deep penetration and specialist targets by night. And it was also realised that the heavy bomber was totally unsuited to daylight operations if it wished to stand a reasonable chance of survival.

August 1942 witnessed the formation of the Pathfinder Force (PFF) under Air Cdre D.C.T. Bennett, with its headquarters at Wyton. No 7 Squadron and its Stirlings became one of five founder squadrons of this new target marking force, and flew its final operation as a Main Force unit on 17 August before joining the PFF.

Wg Cdr H.R. Graham took over from Wg Cdr Paul Harris as CO of No 7 Squadron on 13 April 1941 and played a full part in the daylight 'circus' operations of the early summer against targets in France and the Low Countries. Graham finally gained a staff appointment at Bomber Command HQ, High Wycombe. *IWM CH4471*

In order to increase the Stirling's operational ceiling, Bennett ordered the removal of heavy armour plating in the cockpit, and from the bulkhead dividing the wireless operator's and flight engineer's stations from the cockpit coupe. A reduction was made in the amount of machine gun ammunition carried after it was revealed that many gunners returned from ops with several thousand rounds of unspent ammunition. Bennett also reduced the fuel uplift, cutting the fuel reserve from about 23 per cent to 12 per cent. With the substantial weight savings gained, the PFF Stirlings could now operate at heights in excess of 18,000ft.

(No 7 Squadron began to convert to the Lancaster in May 1943, although both Lancaster and Stirling operated alongside one another on the squadron until the latter flew its final PFF sortie on 10 August 1943.)

'Circus' operations: ugly black flak bursts surround No XV Squadron's Stirling I N3658:E as it crosses the French coast en route to the Kuhlman chemical plant at Chocques, a few miles west of Bethune, on 7 July 1941. *IWM C2029*

Two Hurricanes from the heavy fighter escort formate off the port wing of N3658:E on 7 July 1941. *IWM C2028*

Roy Stamp joined No XV Squadron in September 1941 as a wireless operator and flew a tour on Stirlings after which he was screened from ops in July the following year. His first and last ops were rather 'shaky-dos' which he and his crew were lucky to survive.

We took-off from Wyton at 16.20hrs on 25 November 1941, target Brest, on the west coast of France.

'After dropping our bombs over the German warship base, our aircraft was immediately caught and held by a blue master searchlight which was quickly joined by about twenty other white ones. Our captain took violent evasive action by twisting and turning, but we were held for something like about 5 minutes. This was most uncomfortable as we seemed to be the centre of attraction for all the defences in Brest.

During this time we were being shot at by many anti-aircraft and flak guns, some of the shells bursting very close and hitting us. The smell of cordite was quite strong and I could clearly hear the spray of shrapnel on the aircraft:

I was standing in the astrodome and was amazed at the scene laid out below us. This, of course, was our first operation over enemy territory and it looked for all the world like Dante's *Inferno*. In fact, it was so incredible that I literally pinched my leg to make sure I was not dreaming. Orangey-red tracer bullets were shooting up at us from what

Fresh off Shorts' Belfast production line, Stirling I N6091 is pictured at Sydenham in 1941 before delivery to No 7 Squadron on 2 October. In its biggest operation yet, No 7 Squadron despatched 13 Stirlings in atrocious weather conditions on 7/8 November 1941, as part of a 169-strong force to attack Berlin. Twenty-one aircraft failed to return, representing a loss rate of 12.4 per cent; one of those missing was N6091 which crashed at Spijkenisse in Holland, following flak damage. It was one of two aircraft lost by No 7 Squadron that night.

B. ROBERTSON

Above: Pathfinder Force: No 7 Squadron was one of five founder squadrons of the Pathfinder Force in August 1942. Pictured here in May 1943 is the squadron's CO, Wg Cdr Hamish Mahaddie, with the erks of 'A' Flight.

Right: Roy Stamp was commissioned in July 1942 after completing his first tour with No XV Squadron. R. STAMP

Far right: Searchlights weave their dangerous tracery over Düsseldorf.

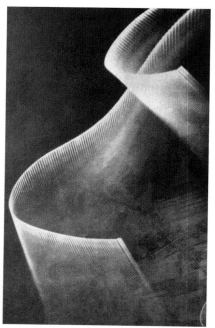

Opposite: Despite its hitherto bad reputation for serviceability, the Stirling played a big part in the first 1,000-bomber raid to Cologne on 30/31 May 1942, with 88 Stirlings despatched by five squadrons as a part of the 1,047-strong force. Pictured at Wyton with Stirling I N3704:A on the day after the raid are Flg Off Neville Bennett and his crew. They were one of the first crews over the target on that historic night, in Stirling N3707, with their flight commander, Sqn Ldr Gilmour, as first pilot (not pictured). From left to right, back to front: Sgt Henry Aldridge, WOp/AG; Sgt Ron Sawyer, flight engineer; Flg Off Neville Bennett, pilot; Sgt Ted Sullivan, WOp/AG; Flt Sgt Ron Johns RAAF, navigator; Sgt Jack Harris, second pilot; Sgt Jack Worley, WOp/AG; Sgt 'Dupe' Dupree DFM, rear gunner. T. SULLIVAN via SAA

seemed like everywhere on the ground, while masses of searchlights all helped to create a fantastic panorama of blazing light.

Finally, our captain decided that the only way to get out of the situation was to put the four-engined Stirling into a very steep dive from our height of about 16,000ft (it seemed almost vertical), lasting for what seemed a very considerable time, then pulling out after having shaken off the searchlights. During the dive, the gravity loadings I experienced made it seem as if my body and feet had left the seat and floor of the aircraft.

As soon as we had levelled out and set course for home, our captain asked me if I was ready to send out an SOS if required. I told him I had anticipated this and written down the callsigns and message for transmission in Morse code.

The port inner engine had been hit and was unserviceable. So was the high-frequency wireless aerial which had been shot away. The aircraft was also hit in a number of other places, but we managed to get back to base. However, this, our first operation, was our worst. Apart from out last operation to Hamburg on 28/29 July 1942. That one WAS our worst.

It was intended to be a 1,000-bomber raid but owing to adverse weather conditions, Nos 1, 4 and 5 Groups cancelled. The remainder comprised No 3 Group (Stirlings and Wellingtons) plus aircraft from the OTUs and HCU – in all, 256 aircraft. However, all the OTU aircraft were

Roy Stamp (far right) poses with his air and ground crews beside Stirling I, W7518 U-Uncle in which they flew an eventful final op to Hamburg on 28/29 July 1942.

R. STAMP

The King and Queen visit No 7 Squadron crews at Oakington in June 1942 after the 1,000-bomber raids. The Queen is talking to Wg Cdr B.D. Sellick. On the right are the King and Grp Capt Adams, the Station Commander. On the left of the picture is Air Vice-Marshal J. Baldwin, AOC No 3 Group, who actually flew on the Cologne raid with a No 218 Squadron crew skippered by Wg Cdr Hodder DFC, the squadron's CO. *B. SELLICK via JR/SBRL*

recalled after take-off, leaving just No 3 Group and a handful of HCU Stirlings to carry on alone, their number amounting to 165. Of these, approximately one-third returned early owing to severe icing conditions.

Although the loss rate for the whole of No 3 Group was 15.2 per cent of the aircraft despatched, in actual fact this rose to 23 per cent of those aircraft which pressed on with the attack.

In our aircraft, U-Uncle, we found the weather particularly bad crossing the North Sea; chunks of ice were continually breaking off from the wings. But we had no idea of the cancellations, recalls and early returns. Difficulty was experienced in reaching the required height owing to icing, but we carried on and arrived over Hamburg just before ETA at something like 17,000ft. There was some cloud about, but this was above us.

As there was no activity in the way of anti-aircraft fire or searchlights, we flew around for some minutes, being puzzled at the quiet scene when we had expected all the usual signs of a very large raid (we were still under the impression it was a 1,000-bomber raid).

I stood in the astrodome and could easily see the Alsters (large and small) and docks. These I recognised as I had been a frequent visitor to Hamburg before the war with my father, who had been a captain on the Grimsby ships which sailed to Hamburg.

Our captain, Bob Phillips, eventually said to Roy Leard, the operator, 'We'll drop our bombs on ETA over the target and then head for home.'

48

Stirling Is of No 1651 HCU formate for the camera during early 1942. W7459 enjoyed a long life with the RAF, originally joining No 149 Squadron on 25 November 1941 and serving thereafter with No 26 Conversion Flight, No 218 Squadron, No 1651 HCU, No 214 Squadron and its conversion flight, before ending its days back with No 1651 HCU, finally meeting its maker on 19 July 1945 when it was SOC. The photograph reveals that the tailwheel doors have been removed, suggesting either accidental damage or problems with the mechanism. *BMIHT*

An unnerving sight at any time: the two starboard engines of a No 1665 HCU Stirling III are feathered during a training flight in mid-1944.

R. GLASS via JR/SBRL

Opposite: A solo pupil pilot who engaged in circuits and bumps on the short runway at Tilstock in June 1944 ran into problems when the very strong wind suddenly dropped during his landing. By good fortune he was able to swing on to the adjacent Whitchurch Road and survive the experience with only a few scratches to the Stirling's undercarriage and tailplaine from the barbed wire fence.

The pupil pilot was not the only one with a charmed life that day. A Jeep loaded with GIs was passing along the road at the time the Stirling made its bid for freedom through the fence. It ended up in the ditch trying to avoid the wayward plane. Originally allocated to No 196 Squadron in late October 1943, Mk III EF210 passed to No 1665 HCU at Tilstock in February 1944 and was written off in an overshoot during an emergency landing on 12 August the same year.

R. GLASS via JR/SBRL

As soon as our bomb doors opened and our bombs were released, the searchlights came on and coned us. Several of these were the blue type. More or less at the same time, the AA guns opened up and began hitting us, in spite of us weaving and corkscrewing. From my position in the astrodome, it appeared as if the whole of the defences in the Hamburg area were being directed at us.

After several minutes of trying to extricate ourselves from this position, our captain put the aircraft into a very steep and prolonged dive. When he eventually pulled the aircraft out of the dive, the searchlights and guns had lost us. We had come down to a very low level and set course for home at something like 50 to 100ft.

As we did not know exactly where we were, the captain and observer decided to fly in a westerly direction at this very low level. I saw many trees going by, and our gunners silenced light flak guns on several occasions when they were firing at us. Our gunners also fired at some searchlights, particularly those we flew directly over, several being extinguished.

We eventually crossed the enemy coast somewhere north of Wilhelmshaven and were soon flying at low level between two of the Friesian Islands. I noticed that the guns on each island appeared to be firing either horizontally or down at us.

After we had climbed to a more normal height, I switched on my transmitter in order to request a fix. As soon as I tapped the Morse key it lit up at the point of contact between the uncovered metal parts, flashing in synchronisation with my signals, as did parts of the aerial – both inside and outside the aircraft. The aerial used when obtaining fixes was of the trailing type, some 200ft long, and it was our gunners who saw these illuminations and asked me what I was playing at. On our return to Wyton, I found that our fixed aerial had been shot away.

After we had landed back at base, the captain pulled back on the control column and found that it had become disconnected from the control runs, so that it just flopped loosely backwards and forwards. There were many holes in the aircraft, some quite large, and next morning in daylight three members of our crew were photographed examining the damaged parts, the picture being published in the *Daily Express*. Our aircraft was so badly damaged that it had to be returned to Shorts for repair.

Our CO asked to see us in his office on the morning following this operation and it was then that he said 'I think it's about time you called it a day and finished your tour'. I came out of his office in a daze. It seemed unbelievable that we had survived for so long and completed thirty ops.

Until the introduction of the new breed of four-engined bomber types like the Stirling and Halifax in 1940–1, novice crews graduated from OTUs equipped with twin-engined Wellingtons, Whitleys, Hampdens and Blenheims, and

passed direct to frontline squadrons equipped with similar twin-engined aircraft. But new types like the Stirling differed from their twin-engined predecessors in their degree of complexity and by the simple fact that they had twice as many engines. They also had two additional crew members: a flight engineer to help the pilot with the increased workload presented by four engines, and a mid-upper gunner.

The problem of converting new crews from twin to four-engined types was solved, initially, by withdrawing a number of aircraft from the squadrons concerned, to form a conversion flight. The first of these was formed in October 1941 when 'C' Flight of No 7 Squadron was hived off to create No 26 Conversion Flight (CF), based at Waterbeach, and which ultimately became a part of the first Stirling Heavy Conversion Unit (HCU) to be formed, No 1651, on 2 January 1942.

But what was going to happen once the first batch of crews to fly the Stirling had been trained on the new squadron aircraft? The whole system would surely fall apart if the squadron had to withdraw most of its aircraft for the training of successive batches of new crews.

Towards the end of 1941, each of the four Stirling squadrons then in existence (Nos 7, XV, 149 and 218) was ordered to form a Conversion Flight of its own for training new crews to operational standard. Each squadron was to make available four aircraft from its own establishment for this task. With the steady increase in the number of four-engined bomber types entering service, it was soon realised that dedicated units would be needed to convert crews from twin to four-engined flying before they could join frontline squadrons. HCUs were formed as the second and ultimate stage of operational training in which pupil crews flew a further 40–45hrs before joining a squadron. A second Stirling HCU, No 1657, opened at Stradishall on 1 October 1942 to cope with the training requirements of No 3 Group's expanding Stirling force.

By May 1943, all eight squadrons had expanded their establishments to three flights due to a combination of sustained production of aircraft and increased throughput of crews from HCUs. Establishments were increased by three aircraft to twenty-four, plus six in reserve, with thirty-three crews. A third HCU, No 1665, was formed at Waterbeach the same month.

The potential for fatal accidents involving inexperienced pupil crews at OTUs and HCUs was alarmingly high. One such instance occurred at No 1651 HCU during May 1943 and involved a pupil crew skippered by Flg Off F.C. Macdonald. The wireless operator, Sgt A.T. Gamble, recalls the occasion on which he almost met his maker:

Perhaps the most exciting thing that happened to us at Waterbeach was when we were taking off for our first night solo circuit. Halfway down the runway, with about 90 on the clock, the port outer seized solid and she started to swing to port off the line of the runway. The choices of action were limited, but Macdonald and the flight engineer, Paddy Martin, wasted no time. The dead engine was feathered, the two inboard engines were slammed into emergency revs and boost, and a great deal of effort was put into straightening out as we became airborne.

The situation then became aggravated by the aircraft changing to a swing to starboard, but we were airborne and the struggle up front continued as we headed straight for the hangars, with not a lot of flying speed to spare.

Many pilots under such circumstances may well have pulled up and risked the inevitable stall, but Macdonald tipped her over to starboard and the wingtip actually passed between two hangars, taking a telephone line with us as we continued in a very low right-hand circuit around the water tower to make a perfect emergency landing.

I think that episode convinced everyone that Macdonald knew exactly what he was doing, and we completed the course successfully to join No 620 Squadron at Chedburgh in June.

By the end of 1942, there were seven squadrons operating the Stirling (Nos 7, XV, 75, 90, 149, 214 and 218), although by January 1943 Bomber Command could muster a daily average of little more than fifty-six Stirlings with crews, against 104 for Halifaxes and 178 for Lancasters. Clearly, the Stirling squadrons of No 3 Group were not making a big enough contribution to the bomber offensive to justify their overheads.

Luftwaffe
Stirling

In the early morning of 16 August 1942, the Luftwaffe became the proud and unexpected second owner of a virtually intact Short Stirling, the first (and probably only) complete specimen to fall into enemy hands.

Following a 'gardening' sortie to German coastal waters in the early hours of 16 August, a No 7 Squadron Mk I, N3705:F, skippered by Sgt S.C. Orrel, suffered engine trouble on the return trip. Rather than risk a sea crossing and the possibility of a ditching, Sgt Orrel decided to land his aircraft in Holland. He pulled off a successful emergency landing with wheels down at about 07.00hrs, in a field near the small town of Gorinchem on the banks of the River Waal in southwestern Holland.

The crew all survived the landing and were rounded up by local troops and eventually ended up as PoWs. The Luftwaffe authorities at the nearby base of Gilze Rijen were alerted to the

After its short flight to Gilze Rijen, N3705 was repaired and repainted before test-flying began. The undersurfaces and lower fuselage were painted yellow, the codes and roundels overpainted in *dunkelgrün*. The cross and swastika national markings were applied, although the aircraft's original serial number was retained. In order to improve its aerodynamic shape, the damaged nose section was fitted with a canvas cover held in place by a tape harness, and padded out with straw.

IWM HU3631

From Gilze Rijen, N3705 was flown to the *Luftwaffe Erprobungsstelle* (Test Centre) at Rechlin on 18 September, escorted by a Dornier Do217 of KG2. The grass airfield of Rechlin was situated amid beautiful scenery at the southern end of Lake Muritz in north-eastern Germany, some 60 miles north-northwest of Berlin. The *E2 Beute* section was in charge of the evaluation of captured aircraft. *IWM HU3626*

A group of intrigued Luftwaffe personnel, from the nearby nightfighter base at Gilze Rijen, examine the cockpit section of N3705 on the morning of 16 August 1942. The damage caused to the nose turret, bomb aimer's compartment and pitot heads is evident. Note, also, how the paintwork on the exhaust collector rings has become chipped with use.

IWM HU3633

Stirling's unexpected arrival. A team of experts under the supervision of Hpt Niemeyer arrived to take a closer look at the aircraft, deciding that it could be salvaged and flown again.

N3705 had sustained only minor damage to its forward fuselage, nose turret and undercarriage during the forced landing. The main wheels had bogged down in the soft ground, tipping the aircraft forward and grazing the underside of the nose. Bearing in mind its reputation for fragility, it is surprising indeed that the stalky main undercarriage remained intact under such rough landing conditions.

Temporary repairs were effected on site, and the aircraft was flown to Gilze Rijen on 5 September for evaluation before flying to the Luftwaffe Test Centre at Rechlin on the 18th. The fate of N3705 is uncertain after this date.

A 'Stirling' Fellow

George Mackie – described as a 'small, dark-haired Scot of serious mien and fiery temper' by Murray Peden in his fine account of wartime life as a pilot on No 214 Squadron, *A Thousand Shall Fall* (Stoddard Publishing Co Ltd) – joined No XV Squadron in June 1941, two months after its re-formation with Stirling Is. By the war's end, Mackie had amassed an almost unbelievable total of over 1,500hrs on Stirlings Is, IIIs and Vs, considerably above the average.

From No XV Squadron he was posted to No 1651 HCU at Waterbeach where he instructed, passing on his already considerable knowledge of the Stirling to the shoals of pupil pilots passing through the training process.

One former groundcrew electrician with No 1651 HCU, Wally Legard, remembers Mackie's reputation at Waterbeach:

> It was a well-known fact among the 'B' Flight ground crews that WO Mackie really relished getting new ground crew erks up on air tests. Of course, not long after joining 1651, I was conned into this.
>
> What WO Mackie didn't do with the Stirlings wasn't worth knowing. Cows and horses raced around the fields in panic as the monster kite hedgehopped over the Cambridgeshire countryside. He even beckoned me up into the cockpit to show me how the wings flapped up and down. He was a demon, but the finest pilot ever to sit at the controls of a Stirling at Waterbeach, and was respected by all the ground crews who knew him.

A return to operational flying came with his posting to No 214 Squadron in late 1943, which converted from the Stirling III to the Flying Fortress II and

Sgt George Mackie, the pilot
(in the foreground), and his
navigator Sgt Cook DFM are
pictured inside one of No
1651 HCU's Stirlings at
Waterbeach in 1942. On the
right of the photograph can
be seen the flight engineer's
panel. *G. MACKIE*

Sgt George Mackie, the pilot (in the foreground), and his navigator Sgt Cook DFM are pictured inside one of No 1651 HCU's Stirlings at Waterbeach in 1942. On the right of the photograph can be seen the flight engineer's panel. *G. MACKIE*

radar countermeasures duties early in 1944. After a further spell of instructing on Stirlings in the autumn of 1944, Mackie joined No 46 Squadron in February 1945 and returned to operational flying with the Mk V in the transport role before he was demobbed in 1946.

They disappeared on their first op, the crew I had trained with, a few days after our arrival at Wyton in June 1941. That was my introduction to No XV Squadron and its Stirlings. The seven of us (including another pilot) had formed up at Bassingbourn flying Wellingtons. We parted company on the squadron because I became second pilot to a crew halfway through their tour while they joined a newly established captain of aircraft halfway through his. At that time a second pilot on board was seen as essential.

Their disappearance passed without comment. It was as if they had never been. They could have had little confidence in themselves as a Stirling crew, having known their pilot, and their aeroplane, for such a short time. I hadn't much confidence myself. I got 2½hrs of desultory instruction before going solo. My logbook showed a total (excluding passenger time) of 150 flying hours. Two years later I had pupil pilots with 400hrs to their credit before they began on four-engined aircraft. I took a Stirling from Wyton, then a grass airfield, to Alconbury, the satellite with runways and a bomb dump. It seemed full of ground crew who would have been less merry if they had known how fragile my confidence was in getting us down safely.

I gave the war little thought for many years. It started coming back to me in the seventies. Reading Len Deighton's *Bomber* helped to spark it off. I began to realise how low morale was in No XV Squadron at that time. I didn't experience anything like it during the rest of the war. It is well known now how ineffectual Bomber Command was in its early years, but the circumstances, and reasons for them, which are clear with hindsight, were then murky and dispiriting. Aircraft serviceability was a constant problem. Bombing was far from accurate, largely because of primitive navigation. And despite the relatively small number of aircraft involved, more than twenty Stirlings were lost during the eight months I was at Wyton. Accidents were also common.

I certainly felt inadequate. I could have done with a little encouragement. Of leadership I recall none. I might have found some in the Officers' Mess. In the Sergeants' Mess I remember only the hostility of peacetime warrant officers, and others, who resented the speed with which wartime aircrew got their three stripes. They seemed unable to recognise how quickly the stripes were lost, along with their owners' lives.

For someone who hadn't even got used to being in the air, the Stirling was daunting. The throttle levers in these early models were parallel and topped off with large red knobs that my hand could scarcely get round. Nor could my feet make full use of the rudder bar, even with the massive seat fully forward. I had to prop myself forward a few extra inches by means of a chest parachute at the small of my back. These were considerable handicaps, given the Stirling's built-in vice of swinging on take-off, which demanded instant, even anticipated response by throttles and rudder to counteract. Accidents on take-off were legion during the Stirling's career. I sometimes wonder if it didn't cause as much havoc to our side as to the enemy's.

After Wyton I spent a long time (mercifully) instructing with No 1651 HCU at Waterbeach, conveniently close to Cambridge. The Stirling's indifferent reputation was becoming well-known and pupil crews used to arrive with varying degrees of apprehension. Take-offs and landings were done by the thousand, day and night, using a score of other airfields in addition to Waterbeach. The worst was Newmarket, which had no runways but enormous grassy hills and hollows creating premature take-offs, and multiple landings. After a year or so in the righthand seat, I did get the measure of the Stirling. What had once been intimidating became a commonplace. I could even make it perform a kind of stall turn, collapsing the artificial horizon, which then spun madly for a satisfyingly long time before settling down again. But skill was also required in such a mundane operation as turning an aircraft around on a circular dispersal point. To avoid strain, the pivoting main wheel had to describe the smallest of circles and not be allowed to turn on itself. The tailwheels then had to run just inside the concrete circumference, whose edge was sometimes sharp, and deep.

'When low-flying, one had to push against the resistance in the control column to get down, down, lower and lower. I have never forgotten the exhilaration of flying across the deserted fens. . .'
IWM CH5496

The Stirling was a responsive aeroplane to fly, provided that bombs weren't stuck on it. We used to believe its liveliness on the controls was due to its ailerons being not far out from the slipstream of the outer engines. It would have been less lively, and more efficient, if its proposed wingspan had not been considerably reduced, at Air Ministry insistence, to allow entry into 100ft-wide hangars. Its nimbleness, unladen and at low altitude, had no military value.

Any take-off (and landing) in a Stirling required care, the more so if there was any wind from starboard. Operational take-offs, with a full load of bombs and petrol, called for the greatest care. Turning onto the end of the runway from the perimeter track, the aircraft is moved forward a little, only enough to straighten the tailwheels. Then, with brakes full on and stick held back, the throttles are opened up as far as possible. The entire airframe begins to judder and vibrate violently, the tail assembly most of all. It takes more strength now to hold the stick back. Then, abruptly, with the hiss of compressed air, the brakes are released, the aircraft surges ahead and the pilot is forced hard back against the back of his seat. At the same time he is now pushing the stick fully forward, to lift the rudder into the slipstream, and pushing the throttles wide open, often diagonally, to counteract any swing. With tail up and rudder control established, stick centred and all engines at full power, the remaining take-off run was simple enough in daylight. The wingtips, previously hidden by the outboard engines, could be seen coming slowly into view as the wings flexed, taking on the aircraft's weight with the wheels bouncing more and more delicately on the runway, on tiptoe, until they lifted clear of the ground. Their spinning was stopped by a touch of the brake, and a large handle, a Heath Robinson affair to the right of the pilot's knee, was pulled out and then up and then pushed in again. A small switch was flicked on, and at last, but not always, the undercarriage began its long, slow, convoluted journey into the inner engine nacelles. The moment it began to move, I throttled back a little. I never liked having the engines at full revs for any longer than absolutely necessary. I kept the climb very shallow, allowing airspeed to build up as quickly as possible. Nothing was more important. With wheels up, power was again reduced and the one-third flap needed for take-off taken in, and trim adjusted. Now the navigator would give the first course and the gyro compass was set accordingly. The night had begun.

We always did three-point landings. Wheeled landings, that is with tail up and a little power still on, were seen as amateur and requiring too much runway. It was a moment of immense satisfaction, returning from a successful op, to put the machine down on the ground so gently that the first indication of it was when the weight of the aircraft rose and fell on the oleo legs of the undercarriage as the landing wheels rolled along the concrete. One of the crew might say 'Good show, skip.' He meant, we live again.

Three-engined landings were common. They were not unduly difficult, nor was an overshoot on three engines. But if the flaps had been fully extended for landing, the aircraft became immensely tail heavy when the engines were opened up. It was then necessary to adjust the highly effective elevator trim tabs to re-establish a balanced trim. When low-flying, I used them so that one had to push against a resistance in the control column to get down, down, lower and lower. I have never forgotten the exhilaration of flying across the deserted fens below the level of their occasional trees. Hitting a bird made a loud bang and could be dangerous. On landing one day after such a strike, with all throttles fully closed, one engine continued to give out an alarming amount of power that lifted a wing in sympathy. Cutting the ignition brought things back to normal. From the uncomplaining ground crew I learned later that a bird had gone into an air intake and fouled a butterfly valve. I was never very happy seeing engines without their cowlings. In their nudity they looked so complicated it was impossible not to believe something, somewhere, would go wrong. As with my entrails, I thought them best out of sight and out of mind.

As well as practising circuits and bumps at Waterbeach, pupil crews and instructors went on 'bullseye' exercises, long night cross-country flights with loaded aircraft. They were supposed to give some semblance of an operational flight. What strikes me as odd (it didn't occur to me at the time) is that on such flights pupil crews were never introduced to the kind of evasive action taken over Germany and Occupied Europe to avoid flak and searchlights. They were certainly given the theory of cork screwing, that helical manoeuvre to present an enemy fighter with the maximum of deflection firing. But when I consider how drastic my own handling of the aircraft became under heavy fire, I believe some such evasive action should have been taught on a 'bullseye', although it would never have been practised as violently as in the heat of actual battle. I used to think that luck alone accounted for one's survival, so many were the skilled and experienced crews who were shot down. I don't think so now.

It could make all the difference between life and death to have the confidence to fling a heavily laden Stirling around the night sky, with a split-second turning dive of perhaps 2,000ft the altimeter needle whizzing round, followed by the gigantic thumpings of the beginnings of a high-speed stall at the bottom of the dive, as the aircraft was pulled up, violently enough, into a steep climb in the opposite direction, to the point where the aircraft was about to stall, this time through lack of speed. I wonder now how the bombs managed to remain secured in the bomb-bay. Evasive action did not prevent you, of course, from flying into a shell burst. But it was, at the least, of psychological value. It was also hard work. One was drenched in sweat. No doubt it was rough on the aircraft too.

For every hour's flying on the Conversion Unit we had the tedium of many hours hanging about in the crew room because of dud weather or unserviceable aeroplanes. Exactor controls gave a lot of trouble at Wyton in 1941. At Waterbeach it was the twin tail-wheels. For no obvious reason they would sometimes begin to shimmy outrageously on touchdown, making the whole fuselage vibrate, often destroying themselves in the process. Some civilian scientists arrived one day to investigate. With them prone in the rear, their faces inches over the tailwheels, I passed an hour or so racing up and down the main runway (the weather was unfit for flying) doing my best to simulate touchdowns and trick the wheels into doing their wobble. I failed; they didn't.

Accidents also enlivened the tedium, not only of hanging around, but of countless take-offs and landings. There was a large steam traction engine parked one day off the end of a runway. Inevitably, a pupil pilot overshot or swung and wrapped his Stirling around it. The following day a second Stirling wrapped itself around the first. We found it all very comical. The memory comes back to me of seeing *MacRobert's Reply*, N6086, swing on take-off from Peterhead airfield in early February 1942. It landed on top of one of the Spitfires stationed there. The runway had been cleared of snow which was heavily banked up on either side. We were part of a contingent from No XV Squadron returning, via Peterhead for some reason, to Wyton from Lossiemouth after an unsuccessful stay. Bad weather had prevented any operations taking place against the German battleship *Tirpitz*, then lying in a Norwegian fjord.

Some accidents were not comical at all. Waiting at the flights for transport to take me and a pupil crew to dispersal on the afternoon of Wednesday 12 August 1942, I watched incredulously, for my brain at first would not admit the eyes' evidence (I remember my knees actually shook a little) as two Stirlings began their take-off runs on different runways. One was tail-high, the other beginning to lift its tail, when they converged at the intersection. The first whacked instantly over on to its back and screeched agonizingly along the concrete, the huge undercarriage sticking up in the air with its black wheels spinning wildly. The other, bereft of the entire nose section and dripping bodies as it went, careered in a wide arc over the airfield with two engines on fire. The aircraft were N6099 and N6127.

With our old and battered ex-squadron machines, we took part from Waterbeach in the so-called 1,000-bomber raids, sometimes with a pupil crew. The one to Hamburg on 28 July 1942 was disastrous. Instead of a maximum effort, only No 3 Group went out; a lunatic decision. The huge amounts of icing cloud over the North Sea were the reason, to my mind, for the loss of four Stirlings out of eight from Waterbeach. None of the four that returned had reached Hamburg. I got back with ten 500lb bombs on board, having jettisoned five others, at intervals, over the sea, in thick and turbulent cloud, in a vain attempt to keep climbing. We were 5hrs 10min in the air. No enemy was involved, yet it was as dangerous an op as I ever made. We were trapped in unrelieved cloud for most of the flight, failing to get above something like 8,000ft. Ice being flung off propellers hit the fuselage from time to time with monstrous bangs. The aircraft was wrapped in ice.

No. 1651 CONVERSION UNIT - BATTLE ORDER - JULY 28th, 1942.

A/C Ltr	CAPTAIN.	2nd PILOT	NAVIGATOR	AIR BOMBER	WOP / A.G.	REAR GUNNER	ENGINEER	M/U GUNNER:
P	P/O Robertson X	P/O O'Hara	P/O Howitt	Sgt Cox	P/Sgt Griffiths	Sgt Young	P/Sgt Prentice	Sgt Fuller
T	P/O Bayley XX	Sgt Lovell	Sgt Spencer	Sgt Wells	P/Sgt Glenwright	Sgt Kilpatrick	Sgt Alder	Sgt Hickman
U	P/O Barron √	P/O Thornton	P/O Frazer	Sgt Clegg	Sgt Allen	Sgt Ward	Sgt Anslow	Sgt Grey
B	F/Lt Parkins XX	P/O Hancock	P/O Thomas	Sgt Robson	Sgt Grant	Sgt Silvester	Sgt Coy	Sgt O'Shea
E	P/Sgt Mackie √	Sgt Ferry	W/O Fisher	Sgt Penham	Sgt Howard	Sgt Clarke	Sgt Watson	
L	P/Sgt Davies X	Sgt Russell Storey	P/O Theobald	Sgt Wilson	Sgt Peters	Sgt Harrington	Sgt Borley	Sgt Teague
G	P/O McGregor XX	P/O Ratcliffe	Sgt Cushnry	P/O Love	Sgt Innes	Sgt Kedwell	Sgt Miles	Sgt Rooney
J	P/O Bird X	P/O Dobson √	Sgt Fossleitner	Sgt Whitehead	Sgt Banks	Sgt Jackson	Sgt Pollitt	
Z	F/Lt Boggis √	P/Sgt Eby	Sgt McNeill	Sgt Trobert	Sgt McKay	P/Sgt Wilson	Sgt Gunton	Sgt Herrity
Q	P/O Smith XX		P/O Breed	Sgt Morrow	Sgt Cox	Sgt Dufour	Sgt Warren	Sgt Aldridge
W	P/O Quinn √		Sgt Richards	Sgt Fellows	Sgt Crodland	Sgt Collins	Sgt Lowrie	Sgt Margetts
R	P/Sgt McCausland. √		Sgt Hammond	Sgt Nixon	Sgt Tree	Sgt Egri	Sgt Busby	Sgt Foster

LOAD: 15 x 500 lbs   PETROL: 1819 Galls.

BRIEFING: In the Briefing Room S.H.Q. at 20.00 hours.

XX Failed to re...
√ Returned e...
X Failed to ta...

(sd) J. Howden.
Flight Lieutenant,
for Wing Commander,
Commanding,
No. 1651 Conversion Unit.

Instrument flying for a long time induces strange delusions. There was sometimes a strong inclination to disbelieve the evidence of the instrument panel and to give in to one's body senses, which demanded imperiously they be obeyed and the luminous, red-lit needles moving ceaselessly inside their circles be ignored. That would have plunged us into the sea.

Four out of eight did. I was debriefed and went to bed. Slept as usual. And as I recall, got up and went about my business that day and on following days as if nothing extraordinary had happened. It wasn't play acting and reaction never came. Unwittingly, I had developed over the months and years, I suppose, a protection of sorts, of blunted sensibilities. It was encouraged by the near silence surrounding losses. They were always abstract. People simply didn't reappear. When things were really bad over Germany, when I saw aircraft exploding or going down in flames, sometimes alongside, my strongest feeling, I have to say, was one of exultation. It wasn't us!

Another specific flight I remember from my mush of operational memories is the 1,000-bomber raid on Essen on 16 September 1942. I had a pupil crew, one of whose number was wonderfully cool and accurate in his fast reporting of the opening up of any blue searchlight.

The Battle Order for No 1651 HCU, 28 July 1942, target Hamburg. The pilot of Stirling 'Z' is Flt Lt Peter Boggis who was at one time skipper of the much publicised No XV Squadron Stirling named 'MacRobert's Reply'. *G. MACKIE*

If caught by such a master beam, one would be coned by its half-dozen subordinate, white, searchlights, and passed on, captive and vulnerable, to the next batch. I never had the experience but I saw it happen often enough. I recall clearly the pleasure of looking down and seeing the blue beam slowly fade out almost as soon as it had come on, proof that our evasive action had allowed us to slide off its radar screen. We managed to repeat the action several times on the last hundred miles to the target. The night was cloudless with no moon, yet it had an extraordinary, luminous clarity.

None of my operational flights was gruesome, which was undoubtedly due to luck, even if I did take every precaution possible. I indulged in no heroics such as going round again on the target, or bombing from 2,000ft, or whatever. I kept as high as I could and never varied the engine revs once we got to our ceiling. I used to wince to hear some pilots talk of engaging the automatic pilot over Germany. To disengage it, a precious half-second of reaction time might be lost. I kept up a gentle, more or less constant, weave over heavily defended areas. I had a horror of fighters getting under us, unseen. By luck or judgement, or both, none ever did. There was a time, not far from Leverkusen in the Ruhr, when we found ourselves on the return flight alone in a clear, peaceful sky. There was no sign of the main stream. We had been late all the way out and now we were taking a short cut. Without warning, we were boxed by umpteen bursts of flak. I felt a gigantic blow on my left arm, so powerful I would have been lifted off my seat but for being strapped in. I dived and twisted out of danger. The night became entirely peaceful again. The engines roared away as before. Nothing vital had been hit. I felt around my arm, which had gone dead. It seemed all there, but absurdly swollen. Of the landing, one-armed as it was, I remember nothing. I imagine Pedro, my South American engineer, must have helped with the throttles.

When the sleeve was cut away, it was found I had suffered nothing more than bruising. Today, where the shrapnel struck looks no more dramatic than another vaccination mark. I have a small jagged chunk of shrapnel which hit my father in 1917. I wish I had been sentimental enough to keep some of the bits and pieces we often brought back in the aircraft.

The only other injury I ever got in over five years of flying was one I gave myself. I gashed my skull and knocked myself out on the way back to the Elsan in a Transport Command Stirling. We were an hour away from Karachi, our destination, at 6,000ft just after dawn. The engineer was at the controls. The fuselage was stuffed full of miscellaneous cargo secured by webbing by means of which I pulled myself through a narrow gap. My head came in violent contact with a sharp edge of the folded-up aluminium escape ladder, fastened to the fuselage ceiling. Tiny stitch marks, no larger than the 'vaccination' mark, are the only evidence today of the incident.

From the haven (relatively speaking) of No 1651 HCU at Waterbeach I was rudely posted back on ops by the station commander, as a punishment for having upset, at a Sergeants' Mess meeting, some peacetime warrant officers. By then I had reached that rank myself, which made me even less acceptable. The following day I was being flown to No 214 Squadron at Chedburgh, a most fortunate posting. It turned out to be a deliverance, not a punishment, because within a short time its Stirlings had been discarded in favour of B-17s, the so-called Flying Fortress. A more docile, a more tractable, a greater contrast to our previous aircraft, could not be imagined. Its four throttle levers fitted the hand like a proverbial glove. It trundled into the air with never a suggestion of a swerve. Its easiness was unnerving after years of coping with the wayward Stirling. In them, packed with radar gear and bristling with aerials of all shapes and sizes pointing in all directions, we accompanied the bomber stream to confuse German nightfighters and their controllers.

The abandoned Stirlings had their own share of radar gear. One was 'Monica', supposed to give notice by means of a series of accelerating beeps in our earphones of any fighter approaching from astern. One very dark night (as black as Tobey's, as wartime slang incomprehensibly had it) at 5,000ft somewhere over the Baltic, at our most vulnerable, straight and level with bomb-bay doors open, we released our cargo of mines. Instantly, and unconnectedly to our startled wits, "Monica" assaulted our ears with frantic beepings. No-one at briefing had thought to mention "Monica's" sensitivity to mines floating out behind, under their parachutes. Nor had we the imagination to anticipate it. We paid with a moment of severe alarm.

Many things one was left to find out for oneself. One night inside thick cloud I watched, startled, as thick lines of blue electricity started flickering between the barrels of the two guns projecting from the front turret. And then, even more startled, I saw perfect circles of blue fire around the tips of all four propellers. The very cloud became tinted with blue reflections.

Returning from the Baltic mining trip, we were diverted to Acklington, north of Newcastle. Many aircraft had been similarly diverted and as we circled the airfield waiting for permission to land, I watched, idly enough, the navigation lights of an aircraft on its final approach. In an instant they vanished, to be replaced by a huge eruption of flames. It was a

Stirling of No 75 (NZ) Squadron which had struck a farmhouse about half-a-mile from the runway. One crew member survived; five children were killed.

In September 1944 I found myself instructing again on Stirlings, this time round in Transport Command. The absence of any nose out front, unlike the Fortress, was particularly noticeable on my first flight. After so many months of flying American, I even discovered the Stirling to be slightly disconcerting to handle compared to the much more stable Fortress. The most agreeable and agile of all Stirlings, the Mk V, I began flying in February 1945 with No 46 Squadron. We transported passengers and freight to and from such exotic (to me, never terrestrially abroad before) places as Cairo, Calcutta and Ceylon. From one of my rare wartime notes I see that with 2,000 revs and plus one boost, we got an indicated airspeed of 190mph. There were no turrets. The finish was silver which seemed glamorous after the tatty matt black and green of Bomber Command camouflage. It was an agreeable way to end my six years in the Royal Air Force. I even fell into a little business arrangement between Tel Aviv and Golders Green whose proceeds cushioned the descent of becoming an art student again, shorn of all status.

I entered the RAF as an immature 19-year-old. I left it scarcely more mature. My experience is that war retards rather than accelerates one's maturing. But my war was abnormal by the standards of history. Even with months of service in the frontline, as it were, I didn't see a single dead body. Nor was I aware of the enormity of Europe's tragedy. I looked down on its burning cities and saw them, with their defences, only as threats to my own survival.

This superb photograph was taken on 30 April 1942 by the famous aviation photographer, Charles E. Brown, from Sgt George Mackie's aircraft, whose shadow can be seen on the starboard wing.

RAF MUSEUM 5929-1 via G. MACKIE

For every Stirling in the air: In order to maintain, service and fly a Stirling, the efforts of fifty-six different people were necessary. To send a typical Stirling squadron of sixteen aircraft on a maximum effort raid to Hamburg in July 1943 required some 26,000gal of 100 octane fuel, 2,050gal of engine oil, 80 × 1,000lb GP bombs, and up to 224,000 rounds of belted 0.303in machine-gun ammunition.

This layout of squadron personnel, shows sectional activities (front to rear):

1. The aircrew — captain, second pilot, air gunner/bomb aimer, flight engineer, navigator, wireless operator and two air gunners.
2. Meteorological officer.
3. WAAF parachute packer.
4. Flying Control officer.
5. Flight maintenance (twelve).
6. Ground servicing (eighteen).
7. Bombing-up team (eleven).
8. Bomb tractor driver.
9. The starter battery is operated by the flight maintenance crew.
10. Oil bowser driver.
11. Petrol bowser driver
    (a corporal) with one AC2. *IWM CH5988*

Late-production Stirling Is fitted with the Frazer-Nash FN50 mid-upper turret are fuelled and prepared for operations at Oakington during 1942. *IWM CH5282*

Sting in the Tail: The four 0.303in Browning machine guns fitted in the Frazer-Nash FN4 rear turret of this early Mk I of No 7 Conversion Flight at Oakington are put through their paces at the firing butts to check for trouble-free operation and correct alignment during early 1942. *IWM CH5208*

The correct working of engines, wireless and radar equipment was checked in an air test early in the day, before aircraft were fuelled and bombed up for the night's operation. In this view of North Creake, photographed in 1944 from one of its resident Stirlings of No 199 Squadron on a morning air test, the eastern perimeter of the newly-completed airfield can be seen with T2 hangars; the watch-tower is towards the left of the picture.
199 REGISTER via JR/SBRL

In this scene of feverish activity, a Matador petrol bowser parked beneath the nose of a Stirling I pumps fuel into the aircraft's fuel tanks – all fourteen of them.

Seven fuel tanks were fitted in each wing, giving a total normal fuel capacity of 2,254gal. For long range targets it was possible to carry three auxiliary tanks in the wing bomb cells on each side, giving an extra 438gal. All the tanks, with the exception of the two inboard leading edge ones (Nos 7), were self-sealing. An oil tank for each engine was fitted in the nacelle in front of the fire wall and held 25½gal (later aircraft held 32gal). *A. LONG via JR/SBRL*

Working in the bomb dump was a dangerous and arduous occupation for those concerned, although the heaviest bombs ever likely to be required on a Stirling bomber station were the 2,000lb HC or AP types. A pile of tail-less 2,000lb HC blast bombs form a dangerous backdrop to these armourers, who are stripped to the waist as they toil away in the bomb dump at Lakenheath in the summer of 1944. *B. CLARKE via JR/SBRL*

Trolleys of Small Bomb Containers (SBC), each of which is filled with 150 4lb incendiaries, are ready to be towed by tractor from the bomb dump to the aircraft dispersals for loading into bomb bays. The Stirling could carry a load of 24 SBCs. *IWM CH6276*

Fused and with its tail attached, this 500lb GP bomb is ready to be taken to the waiting Stirling of No 149 Squadron for bombing up, in the summer of 1943. This particular bomb is fitted with a Type No 30 tail pistol which ensured that the bomb would not detonate too soon if it struck light superstructures or trees on its way down, thus allowing the bomb some degree of penetration before its detonation.

Armourers of Nos XV, 149 and 214 Squadrons were also trained in the handling of chemical weapons, although official documents relating to British policy on the use of chemical and biological weapons during the Second World War would remain under lock and key until well into the 21st century.

B. CLARKE via JB/SBRL

	3 A B	2 A B	1 A B					
	6 A B C D F G H	5 A B C D G H	4 A B C D F G H					
27 A B	26 A B	25 A B	9 A B **X**	8 A B X	7 A B X	24 A B	23 A B	22 A B
	12 A C D E F G H	11 A C F G H	10 A C D E F G H					
	15 A B X	14 A B X	13 A B X					
	18 A B C F	17 A B C D E G H	16 A B C F					
	21 A B	20 A B X	19 A B					

Short Stirling I and III bomb stations and bomb loads.

A: 250lb or 500lb GP or SAP (twenty-seven max); B: SBC stations (twenty-four max);
C: 1,000lb GP (9 max); D: 2,000lb HC (7 max); E: 2,000lb HC with Tails (4 max); F: Mines Type A Mk 1, 1,500lb (6 max); G: 1,900lb GP (7 max); R: 2,000lb AP (7 max); X: These stations cannot be used when heavy type bombs are on stations immediately in front. Note: Seven stations are provided in the main fuselage bomb bay but only six can be utilised owing to centre of gravity limitations.

Source: NOTES AND SKETCH PRODUCED BY NO 218 CF, MARHAM, 19 JULY 1942 FOR HQ NO 3 GROUP

Bomb carriers fitted with electrical release mechanisms and steadying crutches are secured to a group of four 250lb bombs on dispersal at Oakington. The trailer will be manoeuvred beneath the bomb cells of the No 7 Squadron Stirling I and the bombs lifted by a hand-operated winch until the carrier engages with its station in the bomb bay. Crutches are then adjusted to hold the bombs rigid and the firing link is connected.

IWM CH52823/AUTHOR

The port inner of a Stirling III of No 149 Sqaudron receives attention on dispersal at Lakenheath in the summer of 1943. Because of their height from the ground, tall ladders were specially built to enable fitters and mechanics to reach the engines. *B. CLARKE via JB/SBRL*

Fitters check the fuel flow to the port outer Hercules of this No 90 Squadron Stirling III at Wratting Common prior to the Berlin raid of 31 August 1943. The seemingly strange gyrations of the propellers have been caused by the use of a slow camera shutter speed. *IWM CH10923*

Late afternoon on 12 August 1943. You and other Stirling crews of No 149 Squadron at Lakenheath gather for an operational briefing by your CO, 29-year-old Wg Cdr Graham Harrison DFC.

The target for tonight is Turin. This is one of a number of raids you'll be flying this month to Italian targets, designed to hasten the capitulation of Italy (which will eventually surrender to the Allies on 8 September).

The air is thick and heavy with the odorous cocktail of warm bodies packed together, sweet tobacco smoke from the pipes and cigarettes, and the distinctive smell of serge battledress. An air of studied concentration is apparent, each one of you hanging on every word from the briefing officers of what to expect later that night once you have left the shores of England far behind.

Will it be a piece of cake? Will you come back from this one? Of course you will. The chop only happens to other people.

Stomachs tighten and knot. Palms of hands and soles of feet exude cold, clammy sweat. Mouths turn dry. 'Keep your mind on the job,' you tell yourself, trying to blot out the creeping feelings of fear and uncertainty. Keep them buried in that dark corner of your mind.

Utilitarian and unwelcoming, the briefing hut is typical of many which sprang up from the seas of mud at scores of newly constructed bomber airfields across eastern England after the outbreak of war. No quarter was given to creature comforts. *B. CLARKE via JR/SBRL*

Intent on gaining as much useful gen as possible, Sgt North, a navigator with No 149 Squadron, pauses to listen to the final route and target details for the night's work. *B. CLARKE via JR/SBRL*

Individual crews gather round to clarify any outstanding points once the main briefing is over. *B. CLARKE via JR/SBRL*

From a mixed force of 152 Stirlings, Halifaxes and Lancs despatched by Nos 3 and 8 Groups to bomb Turin on the night of 12 August 1943, only two aircraft failed to return – both of them Stirlings. Nearing the target, a No 218 Squadron Stirling skippered by Sgt Arthur Aaron was fired upon and badly damaged by a nervous tail gunner in another Stirling. The navigator was killed, and Aaron, who was fatally wounded in the attack, was posthumously awarded the VC for his devotion to duty.

For Jim 'Red' Gill and his crew in No 149 Squadron's Stirling III EH904 K-Kitty, this was their 13th op. They were attacked by a nightfighter north of Paris on the outward flight and the rear gunner, 'Curly' Mason, was killed. Despite serious damage to the aircraft, they made it back home, where Jack Atkins the wireless op was fined one shilling for failing to wind in his trailing aerial!

Back row, left to right, are: Les Beaton, bomb aimer; 'Curly' Mason, rear gunner. Front row: Harry Cosgrove, navigator; Jack Atkins, wireless operator; Jim 'Red' Gill RNZAF, pilot. *J. ATKINS*

Wg Cdr Graham E. Harrison DFC (second from left) was posted to command the newly re-formed No 190 Squadron in No 38 Group during early January 1944. He was killed in action on 21 September the same year on a resupply drop to the beleaguered 1st Airborne Division at Arnhem when his Stirling was shot down by German fighters. He is buried at Arnhem's Oosterbeek Cemetery.

Harrison is pictured here with his crew at Lakenheath during 1943, beside Stirling III OJ:A. *B. CLARKE via JR/SBRL*

No 7 Squadron, Oakington: Stirlings are marshalled, ready for their crews to join them.
IWM CH5177

The crew bus delivers Dave Oddy and his No 149 Squadron crew to their dispersal at Lakenheath during the summer of 1943.

D. ODDY via JR/SBRL

Len Tonkin and his No 214 Squadron crew prepare to climb aboard Stirling I R9326:U at Stradishall on 1 June 1942, destination Essen, in the second of the so-called 1,000-bomber raids.

D. HORNE via JR/SBRL

A final word from the groundcrew and a snapshot for the album before Flt Sgt John Gow RNZAF of No 149 Squadron prepares to start up at Lakenheath in late 1942. 27-year-old Gow from Southland, New Zealand, was killed on 14 February 1943 in Stirling I W7638:R when it was shot down by a Bf110 near Boxmeer, just inside the Dutch border, returning from Cologne. *J. BRIGDEN*

Plt Off Derek de Rome winds in four divisions of elevator trim in his final pre-take-off checks in Stirling IV LJ566 during 1944:

Rudder tabs:	Neutral
Elevator tabs:	Four divisions forward
Mixture:	Normal
Props:	Speed controls fully up
Fuel:	Check master cocks
Flaps:	One-third out
Superchargers:	Low
Gills:	One-third open
DR Compass:	Normal

N. CHAFFEY

With a look of intense concentration, Flg Off Broadfield eases the throttles forward slowly, the starboard pair leading to counteract the tendency to swing to starboard. . . *C. MUNRO via JR/SBRL*

. . . he gently pushes the control column forward, enough to lift the tail as speed builds, using the rudder to keep her straight on the runway . . . *IWM CH12685*

. . . and eases her off the ground at 110mph IAS, although keeping the nose down to build up sufficient airspeed . . . *IWM CH12686*

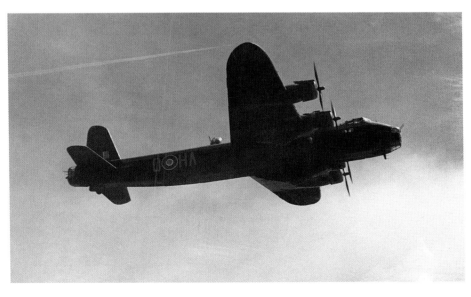

. . . before bringing up the undercarriage and flaps to climb out at 150mph IAS, with the gills one-third open. *IWM CH6310*

Bring on the
Night

With the opening of 1943, the Stirling's credibility as a viable weapon in Bomber Command's inventory of heavy bomber aircraft was in some doubt. On 30 December the previous year, Bomber Harris had written to Sir Archibald Sinclair, Secretary of State for Air, expressing his grave concerns for the Stirling:

> The Stirling group [No 3] has now vitually collapsed. They make no worthwhile contribution to our war effort in return for their overheads. They are at half strength, and serviceability is such that in spite of the much reduced operational rate and long periods of complete idleness due to weather, I am lucky if I can raise thirty Stirlings from 3 Group for one night's work after a week of doing nothing, or twenty the other night. There should be a wholesale sacking of the incompetents who have turned out approximately 50 per cent rogue aircraft from Short & Harlands, and Austins, not forgetting the supervisories in the parent firm.

Indeed, by the end of 1943, the Stirling squadrons of No 3 Group had been withdrawn from Bomber Command's frontline. But before this happened, the year held much in store for them: 1943 saw the introduction of a number of blind bombing, navigational and radio-countermeasure devices which included Oboe, H2S and Window.

The Pathfinder Stirlings of No 7 Squadron received the first H2S sets to be issued to Bomber Command and were ready to use them operationally by the end of January 1943. Bomber Command's strength was also growing, with the formation of No 6 (RCAF) Group on 1 January and the Pathfinder squadrons

Next spread: A Belfast-built Stirling III on a manufacturer's test flight in March 1943. Used initially by No 149 Squadron, BF509 went on to serve with No 1650 HCU before being broken up in 1945.
SHORTS

assuming group status the same month. The number of aircraft deployed for a night's operations began to grow markedly during 1943, with forces of 500, 600 and 700 bomber aircraft pulverising the cities of the Reich by night, compared to maximum effort raids of perhaps 250 aircraft the year before. Albeit in small numbers, Stirlings took part in three of the major night bomber offensives of 1943, the Battles of the Ruhr (March to July), Hamburg (July/August) and Berlin (August 1943 to March 1944). The following accounts by Stirling aircrews of their involvement in the actions of 1943 emphasise that although Bomber Harris may have branded the Stirling as having made 'no worthwhile contribution' to the war effort, the personal contributions made by their crews were second to none.

Just
Good Luck?

As a wireless operator in a crew skippered by Flg Off F.C. Macdonald, Sgt A.T. Gamble joined the newly formed No 620 Squadron at Chedburgh from No 1651 HCU in mid-June 1943, when the Battle of the Ruhr was in full swing and in good time to participate in the devastating fire raids against Hamburg in late July.

The crew flew a full tour of ops, surviving the opening months of the ensuing Battle of Berlin in which Stirling casualties soared to unacceptable levels. Their tour lasted six months, in which time they had taken five freshman pilots on ops as 'second dickies' to acclimatise them to operational flying; by the time the Macdonald crew had been screened from ops at the end of November, all five of these men had been posted as missing.

As summer had given way to autumn, so too had the slashing scythe of the Reaper struck down seventeen of the squadron's Stirlings and crews – the equivalent of an entire squadron establishment.

When the squadron was transferred to the quagmire that was Leicester East on 23 November to join No 38 Group for transport and glider-towing duties, no other crew had managed to complete a full tour. The Macdonald crew was the only one to have started and finished its tour in No 620 Squadron's brief lifetime as a bomber unit.

The eclipse of the Stirlings of No 3 Group by Lancasters was heralded by the transfer of Nos 196 and 620 Squadrons to No 93 Group in mid-November 1943, pending their ultimate consignment to No 38 Group for the duration of the war.

We joined No 620 Squadron at Chedburgh in June and soon got stuck in. Unless it was unserviceable, we flew our own aircraft – 'W' – and finished our tour in November, although the last op was with another 'W'. In that time we had our share of excitement on both bombing and mining sorties.

We did all four of the Hamburg trips among many others and in one period we did three consecutive nights. Throughout the period the

squadron had some heavy losses; on two occasions three aircraft failed to return from the night's operations.

On one of the Hamburg operations our mid-upper gunner blasted away at a shadow that swept in close before he identified it as a Halifax and we learned later that he had injured the flight engineer in the foot, but in such circumstances it was a case of shoot first and ask questions afterwards. I will never forget the night we struggled through perhaps the worst storm that I have ever experienced with St Elmo's fire flickering around all over the aircraft for a long time.

We had a very close shave on 10 August, the target Nuremberg. We were on the bombing run when the mid-upper gave urgent instructions for evasive action and it was just as well Mac responded instantly. I was in the astrodome and scanned around to see what it was all about and there was a Lanc no more than 100ft above us and sliding diagonally across with a 4,000lb cookie just leaving its bomb-bay. We actually felt the displacement of air buffet the aircraft as it passed just a few feet from us between the mainplane and tailplane.

We did our bit on Peenemünde – the rocket research establishment up on the Baltic coast – on the night of 17/18 August. Things were just beginning to warm up when our wave arrived. Fortunately, the rear gunner, Sgt McIlroy, spotted something that was creeping up on us that was not one of ours and both he and the mid-upper let rip as we went into evasive action. They sent a Dornier Do217 nightfighter down in flames before we bombed and went like hell for home down on the deck.

Our worst encounter with searchlights occurred over Berlin on 23 August when the radar-controlled blue master light locked on to us and a good many more chased us around the sky for a long time until we wriggled out of the net. It was all very lively and noisy at the time.

On the 30th we had a unique experience of starting one engine with the starting handle after the starter motor stripped. Quite an experience cranking that 20ft-long monstrosity, but it started and we went, although there was a little more excitement to come. As we approached the target the rear gunner fired at an Me109 that was sneaking up on us and that spun away pouring smoke and flame although we lost contact with him so could only claim a possible.

We set off for Berlin in EF117:W on the 31st but the rear guns went u/s so we returned, although not necessarily aborted. We diverted via the island of Texel and, having woken up the gun batteries, gave them a present of our bombs although we actually got a hell of a strip torn off us on our return. On that night 613 aircraft were despatched, 106 of them Stirlings, seventeen of which failed to return.

Opposite: Safely home: earnest expressions and a few tired jokes echo the dramas of the night's op, as crews of No 199 Squadron relate their experiences to Lakenheath's intelligence officers in late 1943.
199 REGISTER via JR/SBRL

How Some Came Back: This was the damage sustained by No 218 Squadron's Stirling III BK650 at low level over Germany on the night of 14/15 April 1943.

For the night's raid on Stuttgart, a new technique to confuse enemy radar was employed whereby Lancasters flew at 20,000ft, Halifaxes at 10,000ft, and the poor Stirlings went in on the deck, with orders to climb to their bombing height just before the target was reached.

Sqn Ldr Geoff Rothwell, the pilot of BK650, told his gunners that anything which moved at night in Germany was fair game, so they shot up trains, barges and anything on the roads as they made their way to Stuttgart.

Geoff's attention was momentarily distracted by the front gunner's attack on a moving train below when a large electricity pylon loomed up in their path. Geoff managed to pull the Stirling up in a steep avoiding climb, but the bottom of the aircraft caught the pylon, ripping a 6ft section off the bomb-bay. Vivid blue sparks and flashes shot from a transformer station nearby and the crew added to the chaos by jettisoning the incendiaries which had caught fire in the bomb-bays. As if this was not enough, after they had turned for home they were attacked by two Ju88s, but these were driven off.

They managed to reach Downham Market safely and, after landing, discovered the hole in the bomb-bay and nose, and the fuselage from the port inner engine nacelle down to the rear entrance door looked as if it had been opened up with giant shears.

BK650 was repaired and went on to complete twenty-four ops before it was lost on a raid to München Gladbach on 30 August 1943, shot down by a nightfighter near Dorplein, Holland. *G. ROTHWELL via SAA*

We flew a number of ops to targets in Italy. On two occasions returning from Turin in the early hours of the morning we played it safe and got down on the deck to cross France and did a little strafing of opportunity targets that presented themselves. On a raid against the Modane Tunnel in the Alps on 16/17 September we shared the same experience as all Stirling crews did – 14–15,000ft in the moonlight weaving through the mountain tops. Although the bombing instructions intended the bombs to be placed into the valley wall to bring enough debris down to block the tunnel, we did it differently. The bomb aimer could not get lined up so we went around again. Literally! We went down into the valley which was only three miles across the top, did an about-turn and placed the bombs in the tunnel mouth although it did mean flying under the incoming main stream and a lot of twisting and turning before we could get out of it. When we did, another target presented itself – a convoy on the Italian side which we blasted into until nearly all our ammunition was gone. I think on that occasion we made a fairly substantial contribution to the war effort but, I have to say, we did not report it. It was better that way.

Kassel was the target on 3 October and we were obliged to take EE971; the port inner engine failed even before we crossed the coast outbound. It was the third trip in a row where we had suffered an engine failure

This official poster, produced by the MAP for display on the walls of factories in the Stirling production group, needs little explaining. *JR/SBRL*

STIRLING BULLETIN No. 13.

FLYING LOW IN MOONLIGHT, GOING TO STUTTGART, A STIRLING COLLIDED WITH AN ELECTRIC PYLON NEAR A BIG POWER STATION.

BROKEN WIRES FILLED THE AIR WITH BLUE FLASHES AND THE STIRLING'S FUSELAGE WAS STABBED AND GASHED UNDERNEATH WITH HOLES. THE INCENDIARIES IN ITS BOMB-BAYS CAUGHT FIRE...

HASTILY THE PILOT JETTISONED HIS LOAD, SET COURSE FOR HOME AND MADE A SAFE RETURN.

THAT AIR-CREW WILL NOT FORGET WHAT THEY OWE TO THE BUILDERS OF THEIR STIRLING.

MINISTRY OF AIRCRAFT PRODUCTION.

Airframe: B.K. 650

Engines: Port outer: SS 6202/A.308110   Star. outer: SS 6336/A.308244
       „ inner: SS 6424/A.308332   „ inner: SS 6268/A.308176

and Mac was a bit wound up about it, deciding to press on. The rest of us had no choice. We bombed the target and headed for home by the most direct route to save fuel which we had been using at an alarming rate and continued to use at a high rate to get maximum speed. Over the Channel we jettisoned as much weight as possible. Ammunition was fired off and we prepared for a possible ditching, but we made our own coastline, heading for Tangmere, as the engineer and navigator got their heads together with fuel states and flight times. It was not one of Mac's best decisions to fly on to base with only a 5min margin of fuel. Mac had the bit between his teeth as the rest of us were putting our parachutes on and not without good reason. Another engine died through fuel shortage despite the fact that all the tank cross-feeds were open. The engineer goofed and feathered the wrong one and we were descending like the proverbial brick lavatory as we made for an illuminated airfield while I fired off everything in the cartridge rack. In order to keep the speed up, Mac stuffed the nose down and we lost 5,000ft very rapidly. There was not much more to spare as we pulled out on the final approach and flared out to touch down on one good engine and one spluttering. Then we ran out of fuel completely at the end of the runway and everything stopped – except for some very caustic comments and a great deal of bad language. We had landed at Wratting Common.

On 8 October we were off to Bremen in a diversionary force as the main attack was going to Hanover. Heading for the target I was chucking leaflets out of the rear hatch when all hell broke loose with the rear gunner giving orders for evasive action and firing at the same time, being joined by the mid-upper.

With all the noise, sparks and flashes going on around me, plus the fact that we were being hurled around all over the sky, there was only one way I could hit out and that was to throw and kick out the bundles of leaflets; I saw the attacker pass underneath us. The unusual thing was that there were two trails of fire streaming from it and that's how we reported it. Although we were not believed at the time, subsequently I found out that our observations were right.

Meanwhile we were sorting ourselves out as we went on to the target. Despite the fact that we had taken a real hammering, everything was still working. Although the rear turret had jammed, the flight engineer freed it with judicious use of the fire axe and then made emergency repairs to some hydraulic piping in the vicinity of the rear hatch where a hit had sprayed me with splinters and hydraulic oil. Nevertheless, we stayed in the stream, bombed and returned, making some very careful checks on everything before we landed.

The aircraft was a mess with hardly a square foot without a hole in it. The rear turret had lost most of its perspex and its doors. The well of the turret had holes you could put your fist through. The rear bulkhead door was splintered and the rear gunner's parachute pack in its stowage was full of holes. The area where I had been sitting was peppered with holes and the step over the back end of the bomb-bay had a neat group of five holes. Had I not jumped up when I did, I would have collected that lot in a most vital spot and I doubt if I would have subsequently raised a family. There were scars and scorch marks everywhere and the glass of some of the cockpit instruments had been broken, but what was most extraordinary was that no-one had a scratch – not even the rear gunner whose 6ft 2in frame filled the turret and whose boots, trousers and jacket were all nicked around the edges.

Fifteen years later while serving in Amman, Jordan, I heard the other side of the story from the ex-Luftwaffe pilot himself who, prior to having a go at us, had already shot down two Stirlings that night and was out of cannon shells. He was quite convinced at the time that we would never get home if the amount of debris that had flown back at him was anything to go by. In actual fact it wasn't debris, it was leaflets! Apart from the holes, we were intact, but bad enough all the same to need some major repair work, so EF433 was replaced with EF189. EF433 never went back on ops again; she subsequently went to No 1665 HCU as OG-N and someone else wrote her off with a 'swinger'.

The conversation with that ex-Luftwaffe pilot did confirm one thing, though: it was a jet that had got us and our report may well have been one of the first to report the existence of the German jet.

That was nearly our swan song. We took our new 'Willie' out on 3 November for mining in the Kattegat between Denmark and Sweden, but just after we had dropped our mines a flak ship let loose at us and as we started wriggling all over the place an Me109 got on our tail. From then and for the next half-hour we wriggled and twisted and turned as we played tag with the 109 at very low level across Denmark, around pylons and chimney pots with some very intensive conversations between the gunners and pilot. The 109 fired several bursts at us, all wide, and since Mac's instructions were not to fire until we were absolutely certain of getting him, we spent more effort in evading and never fired a shot until eventually the 109 sheared off, either alarmed at being so low level at night or running short of fuel.

Needless to say, the poor navigator's plot had suffered to the extent that he hadn't a clue as to our exact position. Both the magnetic and gyro compasses had been badly affected and were unreliable. We picked up a bit of height but we were still too far out for Gee to be very effective

and Mac had imposed radio silence, so I was unable to call the UK direction-finding service. We staggered around until at one time we figured that with the moon in a certain place and an illuminated coastline we must have been heading for Sweden. After several hours of navigation by rule of thumb and some very doubtful astro shots, the bomb aimer reported a visual fix – the east side of the Zuider Zee – and would confirm it when the west side came up. How wrong he was! As we came up to Dover, about thirty searchlights – and it seemed as many guns – pinpointed us with the arrival of a massive salvo that sprayed shrapnel all over us and bounced us into the air while the pilot started to throw us around, bellowing over the R/T. I threw the IFF switch and started firing off the colours of the day as rapidly as I could fire and reload. Fortunately they got our message and that was the only salvo we got. It was enough, though. We got back to base and landed safely, although our underside was somewhat shredded and another 'Willie' was consigned to the repair depot.

After being screened from ops I spent just over a year instructing and then went back on Lancs, but after having had to bale out of one with only half a wing on the starboard side, I finished the war as a guest of the Third Reich.

Nightfighter Victim: On 26 April 1943, Stirling III BF517 O-Orange, of No 75 (NZ) Squadron, was attacked from astern by a nightfighter north of Duisberg. The rear gunner was fatally wounded and the aircraft seriously damaged. The 19-year-old pilot, Plt Off P. Buck RNZAF, and the navigator, Plt Off J. Symons RCAF, nursed the crippled aircraft back home to a successful crash-landing at Newmarket. Both men were awarded immediate DFCs.
IWM CE58

Visions
of Hell

J ames McIlhinney, an Ulsterman, had trained as a navigator, and it was Christmas 1942 when he arrived at No 12 OTU at Chipping Warden, Oxfordshire; it was fast approaching midsummer 1943 by the time he and his all-NCO crew had graduated from No 1651 HCU at Waterbeach in the county of Cambridgeshire, to join No 218 (Gold Coast) Squadron at Downham Market, Norfolk:

> During the spring and early summer most operational trips were to the Ruhr Valley – 'Happy Valley' to us. Very soon we appreciated that we were in a bitter battle against the German defences of flak, searchlight

New Boys: Flg Off McAllister and crew, weighed down with baggage and thoughts of what may lie ahead, arrive at Downham Market railway station at the start of their posting to No 218 Squadron. *A. LONG via JR/SBRL*

Navigator: WO 'Busher' Bush
of No 199 Squadron
navigates with his Gee chart
in front of him and Dalton
Computor by his side.

C. MUNRO via JR/SBRL

batteries and nightfighters. The Ruhr Valley was very strongly defended – my navigation chart had huge red areas of heavy defences marked on it – areas we attempted to bypass on our route into and out of the target.

During those spring months we bombed Essen, Dortmund, Düsseldorf, Cologne, Aachen, Krefeld, München Gladbach, Duisberg, etc, relentlessly. Losses were heavy but our morale remained high, partly I think because we tended to live within our own crew, not having strong ties with more than a few outside.

My memories are like a kaleidoscope, shifting from one scene to another. The banter and slightly strained laughter in the ops room as we gathered and waited for the target to be revealed, crews jostling with one another; the silence as we shuffled to our feet as the group captain and his cohorts came in; the indrawing of breath as a sticky target was announced. This was followed by instructions on tracks to be followed, turning points, track markers and target indicators. The met officer had his say, the armaments officer told us the bomb load, the signals officer briefed the wireless operators; fuel loads, intelligence reports on

A victim of the Stirling's frightening tendency to swing on take-off, No 218 Squadron's Mk I EF353 swung on take-off for its 14th op on 17 May 1943. An engine cut and she slewed out of control into the station's ops block, overturning the Group Captain's car in the process. Surprisingly, EF353 lived to fly another day, passing to No 1657 HCU before it was SOC on 15 August 1944. *J. McILHINNEY*

Hamburg, 27/28 July 1943: On this, the second of the fire raids, 729 RAF aircraft rained 1,464 tons of high explosive and 975 tons of incendiaries on the city, which was then engulfed in a terrifying firestorm. The freak combination of hot weather, low humidity, accurate bombing and the fact that the fire brigade was still dealing with the results of the 24/25 July raid in the west of the city, proved disastrous. The ensuing firestorm killed over 40,000 people. It was some six weeks before what bodies were left had been recovered. This photograph was taken as the raid was developing shortly after 1am, and shows the Wandsbek district of the city which was very shortly to be engulfed in the cataclysmic firestorm. A: Horner Weg; B: Washington Allee; C: Kamp Jenfelder; D: north end of Stengele Strasse; E: incendiaries burning among barracks; F: fires in the grandstands of the racecourse. *IWM C3832*

FORM 4

SQUADRON _218_   A/C NUMBER _F.J 112_   LETTER _Z_   DATE _24.7.43_

CAPTAIN _Sgt Hamilton_   NAVIGATOR _Sgt McIlhinney_   2nd PILOT B/A _Sgt Ashton_

CREW _Sgts Harrison, Jackson, Martin, Halan._

SPECIAL ORDERS _Ops - Hamburg. Take off 22.35. s/c 22.49. Eng coast out 22.55._
Enemy out 01.01. TARGET 0122 - 0126. Enemy back 0159.
Eng back. 0340. Base 03.55. Zero Hour 01.00.
Convoy 25 miles E of Track 0800.

	SUN		MOON		TWILIGHT	
	RISES	SETS	RISES	SETS	A.M.	P.M.

WATCH _20 secs_ Fast **Slow** RATE _½_ secs./hour Gaining **Losing**
AT _1500_ **BST** G.M.T.

FROM TO	W/V USED	HEIGHT FT.	T.A.S.	RQD. TRACK (T)	COURSE (T)	VAR.	COURSE (M)	D.R. G/S	DIST.	TIME
BASE / CROMER	315/5	4000'	160/170	061°	059° 235°	10°W	069°	171	45	16
CROMER / 54°45'N 07°00'E	315/5 · 310/9	4000' / 10,000	170/186	061°	059°	8°W	067°	171 173 92	60½ 20½	
54°45'N 07°00'E / 53°55'N 09°45'E	315/15	16000	165/208	118°	117°	6°W	123°	128 124	33½	
53°55'N 09°45'E / TARGET	315/16	16000	189/228	157°	159°	5°W	164°	242 26½	6½	
TARGET / 53°15'N 10°00'E	315/15	16000	180/234	180°	183°	5°W	188°	238	22	5½
53°15'N 10°00'E / 64°30'N 06°00'E	315/5 310/12	14000'	228/234	298°	299° 299°	6°W	315°	212 222	120 65	34 17½
54°30'N 06°00'E / CROMER	310/8	8000'	190/215	240°	241°	9°W	251°	212	218	62
CROMER / BASE	315/5	2000'	180/186	241°	243°	10°W	253°	183	45	15

FORECAST WINDS

STAGE	FROM TO	2,000 FT.		5,000 FT.		10,000 FT.		15,000	
		FROM T.	SPEED	FROM T.	SPEED	FROM T.	SPEED	FROM T.	S
ALL STAGES		NW	5-10	NW	5-10	210	10	310	

WEATHER FORECAST

Form 2330 carried
Red - Sea 54°34'N .07°40'E
Yellow - Coast 54°12'N .08°50'E
Y, R, G on target

(R - G)

32

The navigator's log compiled by Sgt James McIlhinney on the first Hamburg fire raid of 24/25 July 1943. *J. McILHINNEY*

nightfighters and flak concentrations, the bombing run, and finally we were given a pep talk on how important the target was and to avoid creep back on our bombing.

Of these operations to the cities in the Ruhr my memories are an amalgam of ferocious struggles with the enemy nightfighter forces and the searchlight and flak batteries. On the bombing run I usually doused my navigation table light, opened the curtains separating me from the pilot and clambered into the second pilot's seat vacated by the bomb aimer who was now in the bomb aiming compartment. The sight that met me on those occasions will never fade from my memory: the huge fires, blossoming and belching outwards, black smoke towering up for thousands of feet, the huge bubbling explosions of 4,000lb bombs, the myriad tiny pinpricks of light where incendiaries were creating new fires. Searchlights scoured the sky, cones of searchlights in their twenties, thirties, forties, exposing a bomber like a dragonfly in their brilliant light. Flak seized on such with frightening speed and accuracy and anyone escaping from a searchlight cone was fortunate. Flak bursts were

TIME	RQD. TRACK (T)	W/V USED AND D.R. DRIFT	Course (T)	Course (M)	NAVIGATIONAL OBSERVATIONS (Pin-points, Fixes, Position Lines, Actual T.M.G., Actual Drift, G/S and W/V, Manoeuvres, etc.)	GENERAL OBSERVATIONS (Met. Conditions, Bombing, Intelligence, Enemy Action, etc.)	R.A.S.	HEIGHT & A. TEMP.	T.A.S.	D.R. G/S	DIST. TO RUN	D.R. TIME	E.T.A.
22.10					WATCHES SYNCHRONISED	VERY LOADED JETS IN							
22.25					TAXYING OUT	ICE ON, COMP SYNCH							
22.42					A/B BASE	OXYGEN ON							
22.50	061°	315/15 295?	059°	069°	BASE S/C CROMER	NAV LTS OFF DR CHECKED GROUND HAZE ABOVE & BELOW	160	4,000	170	171	45	16	23.0
23.06					FIX 52°48'N 1°00'E DIST 285'? G/S 171	CLOUD - NIL				170	171	17	6	23.06
23.06					CROSSING ENG. COAST	CONVOY SIGHTED N OF TRACK 23.11 IFF OFF							
23.06	061°	315/15 295?	060°	060°	CROMER a/c 5°00'E		160	4,000	170	171	173	60?	00.06
23.10			36°		a/c 36°(T) TO AVOID CONVOY	CONVOY PORT BOW - 23.08							
23.17			059°	067°	RESUMED TRACK								
23.17					FIX 53°08'N 01°54'E W/V 337/12 AIR PLOT	CLOUD 4/10 ON SEA INCENDIARIES JETTISONED				171	144	5½	00.02?
23.29½					FIX 53°22'N 02°37'E W/V 372/10	ON PORT BOW - 23.15 REQUEST LOOPS H, B, C - 23.30				171	70	24½	00.06
23.41					FIX W/V 316/12 AIR PLOT								
23.48					B1 - 156° - 1ST - 23.39 = 158 + 061 - 180 = 039 TO PLOT C2 - 202° - 1ST - 23 40 = 202 + 061 - 180 = 083° T								
23.57					FIX 53°55'N 04°22'E (VISUAL AIR PLOT)								
00.07	057°	315/15 5°S?	054°	061°	DR 54°00'N 05°07'E a/c POSTN A	CLIMBING ON TRACK	155	10,000	190	182	88	29	00.36
00.16					POSTN LINE CUTS TR 54°06'N 05°43'E	VSC checked							
00.20					POLARIS H° 54°49'E → 54° 23'N - TO PLOT								
00.26	115°	315/15 5°S?	119°	122°	DR POSTN A a/c POSTN B	2 AIRCRAFT ST/BEAM 00.32 00.33 ENCOUNTER FIGHTER	165	16,000	208	227	124	35½	01.0?
00.33					REAR GUNNER OPENS FIRE - CORKSCREW								
00.36					ENGAGEMENT BROKEN - HOLED DRAUGHTY								
00.45					Yellow T.Is ahead					277	222	87	27½	00.55
00.50					FIGHTER PORT ½ ATTACKED -					210	124	35½	01.14
00.54					Y. T.Is 2 MILES STARBOARD (restart airplot)	VSC checked	180	16,000	195	242	265	6½	00.57 +2C/n 01.0
01.05	157°	315/15 24R?	159°	165°	Mr POSTN E a/c TARGET	VIS. FAIR - HAZY CONES OVER TARGET 30-50 IN EACH							
01.16					CONES S/LIGHTS ON KIEL CANAL 30								
					TARGET AHEAD T.Is GREEN & RED	COLUMN SMOKE 10,000' HIGH							
01.18½					BOMBS GONE H/1200/T IAS 190 HT 16000	AIRCRAFT CONED - 01.19 SHOT DOWN. PARACHUTES SEEN							
01.19	180°	315/15	153°	133?	TARGET a/c POSTN C	bags of S/LIGHTS	180	16000	210	288	22	6	01.2?
01.20					CONED, BAGS OF FLAK. Violent evasive action PORT OUTER IN FLAMES OK - FEATHERED, OUT OF CONE - DAMAGE SEVERE		120	16000 215/-30		184	185	60	02.25
01.25	298°	315/15	299°	315°	POSTN C a/c 'D'					184	65	21	01.46
01.35					Yellow T.Is ahead	green flares Starboard				184	116	38	02.20
01.42					5 MILES STARBOARD INCREASE. IAS 180	cloud 6/10th's low patches	180	14000	215	200	63	19	01.19
02.00					LEFT OVER FRISIANS. a/c SHOT DOWN CUXHAVEN								
02.02													
02.17					enemy fighter sighted port 8°C - OK								
02.22	240°	310/10	247?	251°	DR POSTN D a/c CROMER	VSC reset comp synch	180	7000	200	71 218	62	02.2?
02.35					FIX 54°28'N 05°16'E (restart airplot)								
02.47¾					POLARIS H° + Q corren = 54°03'N				170	3000	178			
02.54					IAS 170								
02.55					FIX 54°?'N 02°45'E 116 3200 Drift 6°? G/S 190 W/V 300/12 T & G/S W/V 302/10 AIR PLOT	IFF ON COMP SYNCH							
03.05	230°	300/12 4°P?	234°	243°	DR 53° 40'N 03°?'E a/c CROMER	LOOPS REQUESTED	170	3000	178	171	92	34	03.39
03.15					C2 - 077° - 1ST - 03.12 + 234° = 261 - 180 = 081° TO PLOT D1 - 005° - 1ST - 03.13¼ + 234 - 22? - 180 = 059 TO PLOT								
03.22					FIX 53°24'N 02°00'E W/V 308/8? AIR PLOT	VSC check							
03.35	230	302/8	229	239	DR 53°03'N 01°14'E a/c BASE	IFF check	170	3000	178	187	44	14	03.4?
03.41					FIX 52°56'N 00°58'E					197 132	33	11	03.7?
03.51					BASE entering circuit	Bomb unloaded IFF OFF JETS OUT, OXYGEN OFF							
04.42					LANDED								
04.50					CHOCKS UNDER								

everywhere and in this glowing red cauldron one could see other bombers, Stirlings, and above us Lancasters, either early or late in their bombing run. It was awesome and terrible.

As a navigator, going to and coming from the target, I was isolated in my lit compartment bent over my log and chart, curtained off from the pilot and the outside world, and too busy to be greatly concerned about what was going on outside. It was only when the aircraft suddenly shuddered or rose and fell rapidly on running into the disturbed air from a flak burst or another aircraft's slipstream that I became acutely aware of our vulnerability. Of course, when attacked by a nightfighter I hastily seized my pencils, dividers, protractor and nav computor; everything that was loose as the pilot threw the aircraft into violent evasive action on the alarm given by the rear or mid-upper gunner. There followed the rattle of gunfire with its attendant acrid smell, the gunners' language graphic, descriptive and not overly polite, and frequently the action was over as quickly as it began.

Damage from flak and nightfighters was frequently sustained but the Stirling was a sturdy machine and many came back with huge chunks torn out of them – damage that would have downed a lesser aircraft. Even though we were aware that our bomb loads were less than those carried by the Lancaster and that we operated at a height that was 6–10,000ft lower than they, we felt pride in our Stirlings, reckoning that our bombing was much more accurate.

A raid that remains very much in my memory was the first Hamburg raid on 24/25 July 1943 when 'Window' was used for the first time. When we were told at briefing about 'Window' and how to use it, we were inclined to be sceptical at the predictions of it confusing the enemy's radar-controlled guns and searchlights.

Hamburg had been attacked ninety-eight times already since the outbreak of war and maximum effort was called for against Europe's largest port and Germany's second largest city. A force of 791 aircraft, of which 125 were Stirlings, left the shores of England to strike the first of four massive body blows to the city in the space of ten nights, culminating in a cataclysmic firestorm on the second raid that claimed the lives of about 40,000 people.

James McIhinney and his crew took off at 22.40hrs in Stirling III EF410:Z, skippered by Sgt N. Hamilton:

It was a beautiful summer evening when we took off, and soon over the eastern counties of England, like a swarm of gnats, bombers circled and climbed, setting course for the coast and the long haul across the North Sea to a turning point off the coast close to the Danish border. The short summer night drew in but we were aware of the vast concourse of aircraft heading northeast. Some distance from the coast, Window was dropped and continued as we crossed the German coast to a turning point where we turned south to the city of Hamburg.

The task of pushing the bundles of aluminised strips down the flare chute was shared by the bomb aimer and flight engineer, an unenviable job as they came back with blackened faces and hands, grumbling about the cold and discomfort of crouching at the back of the fuselage, feeding the flare chute with the bundles of Window which sometimes burst open and a back-draught would carry them helter-skelter all over the interior.

As on other trips I climbed into the second pilot's seat but this time I was astounded at the different reception we received: searchlights were uncoordinated, moving aimlessly around the sky. We knew Hamburg was heavily defended but the searchlight batteries were completely confounded by Window, leaving individual searchlights to search blindly. Flak was no longer controlled by radar and instead relied on a box barrage.

Hamburg is a big city, but a large section of it was heavily hit; huge fires blazed, high explosive bombs burst like black mushrooms, something like shockwaves being visible around each. Flak was heavy, but above us, and we were unscathed.

Flg Off M.W. Nesbitt and his crew were one of several taken from No 218 Squadron's 'C' Flight to form No 623 Squadron on 10 August 1943, as a part of the expansion of the Stirling force. The new squadron played only a minor part in operations before its disbandment on 6 December the same year, to provide aircraft for a conversion unit.

Stirling III BF568 stands in the background bearing the 'IC' Squadron codes of No 623 Squadron. It passed successively to No 214 Squadron and No 1651 HCU before being SOC on 24 April 1945. *A. LONG via JR/SBRL*

Survivor: Flg Off Cedric Eyre was the only man to survive from Wg Cdr Don Saville's No 218 Squadron crew, when they were shot down over Schleswig-Holstein by a nightfighter on the 24/25 July raid. *G. ROTHWELL via JR/SBRL*

Our route out was between Bremerhaven and Cuxhaven, both heavily defended, but Window proved to be every bit as effective as we were told at briefing. We were many miles at sea before we lost the fiery glow of Hamburg burning behind us. Our elation was short-lived: even though our losses were extremely light, something about ten or twelve I think, our squadron commander Wg Cdr Saville had not returned. He was into his second tour of operations, and we all felt his crew's loss deeply. Morale dropped for a few days, but we were all young and soon his loss was put behind us.

Indeed, the losses for the night were very low: twelve aircraft, of which three were Stirlings, representing a loss rate of 1.5 per cent for the entire force despatched.

Flying in Stirling III BF567, Wg Cdr Don Saville DSO, DFC, the 39-year-old Australian CO of No 218 Squadron, and most of his eight-man crew were on the ninth trip of their second tour when they were shot down by a nightfighter, crashing some 40 miles north of Hamburg at Einfeld in Schleswig-Holstein. Flg Off Cedric Eyre, the navigator, was the only man to survive and spent the rest of the war as a PoW in Stalag Luft III.

Bomber Command was to visit Hamburg again on 27/28, 29/30 July, and 2/3 August.

Hitting
Back

Chris Dickenson joined No 75 (New Zealand) Squadron at Newmarket from No 1651 HCU, Waterbeach, in April 1943 at the opening of the hard-fought Battle of the Ruhr, and completed a tour as a sergeant flight engineer with Sgt 'Speedy' Williams' crew before being screened from ops in November, and passing to No 28 OTU to instruct.

Chris Dickenson and crew pictured at Mepal in front of their regular mount, EH936 W-Willy, on 15 July 1943. From left to right: 'Speedy' Williams, pilot; Ivan Kay, rear gunner; 'Shorty' Carson, bomb aimer; 'Taffy' Williams, wireless operator; Trevor Dill, navigator; Chris Dickenson, flight engineer; Bill Hemsley; mid-upper gunner. *C. DICKENSON*

The relief of returning home
safely is evident on the faces
of these No 149 Squadron
crews as they pause for mugs
of tea laced with rum, a
cigarette and a chat, before
debriefing at Lakenheath in
the spring of 1944.
IWM CH12689

Speedy Williams' crew flew on all four Hamburg raids in July and early
August 1943, interspersed with ops to Essen and Remscheid, and the brief
comments in Chris Dickenson's log book reveal something of the drama of those
summer nights:

> 24 July 1943, target Hamburg: 5 x 1,000lb bombs, coned in
> searchlights going in to target. Good prang, heavy flak. Window very
> successful.
> 25 July 1943, target Essen: 5 x 1,000lb bombs. Shot fighter down going
> in to target. Saw E/A [enemy aircraft] blow up and crash in flames.
> Heavy flak, many searchlights. Second fighter attack when leaving
> target, no damage.

The combat report filed by the two gunners, Sgt Bill Hemsley (mid-upper) and
Flt Sgt Ivan Kay (rear gunner), tells the story:

COMBAT REPORT

No 75 Squadron, 25/26 July 1943
Stirling W:EH936, Time: 00.30hrs
Target: Essen, Captain: F/S Williams

Stirling 'W' at a position 52 00N, 06 20E [15 miles E of Arnhem] flying on a course of 130M, visibility good, no cloud, the moon was still down and there were no pronounced Northern Lights. There was no searchlight activity or Track Indicating Lights.

The R/G [F/S Kay] first saw the unidentified single-engined a/c flying at the bomber's height on the port beam 2,000yds away. There was no flak in the immediate vicinity.

The e/a shadowed the bomber for about five minutes closing round via the port quarter to dead astern.

The e/a had a bright white light on the top of the fuselage. The R/G told the pilot to corkscrew port and opened fire with a 3-second burst on the e/a at 400yds. The e/a closed in to 300yds and both the mid-upper gunner [Sgt Hemsley] and the R/G opened fire with a 30-second burst. The e/a did not reply with any fire at the bomber and both gunners observed the e/a blow up in mid-air.

It fell to the ground and the gunners and captain saw it burning on the ground. The e/a is claimed as destroyed.

At 00.55hrs

The same crew on the way home at a position five miles north of Duisberg at a height of 19,000ft flying on a course of 296M with a speed of 200mph (I), were attacked twice by an unidentified twin-engined a/c.

The visibility was good, the moon was low and there were no pronounced Northern Lights.

The e/a was first seen 500yds away on fine port quarter. At this range the R/G told the pilot to corkscrew to port and he opened fire with three short bursts. The e/a broke away to starboard without opening fire but came in again from starboard and the R/G again opened fire at 500yds with two short bursts and told the pilot to corkscrew to starboard. The e/a broke away on the port quarter down and was not seen again, but no hits were observed on the e/a.

There were no searchlights or Track Indicating lights near the bomber during any of the attacks.

Flt Lt Bill Betts and his crew examine damage to the wing flap of their No 149 Squadron Stirling, inflicted by a nightfighter during a mining sortie in the spring of 1944.

IWM CH12690

The crew resumed operations two nights later:

> 27 July 1943, target Hamburg: 20 cans of incendiaries. Many searchlights, light flak, smoke up to 16,000ft.
> 29 July 1943, target Hamburg: heavy flak and many searchlights. Smoke up to 16,000ft.
> 30 July 1943, target Remscheid: 23 cans of incendiaries. Concentrated flak and searchlights. Coned over target. Good prang.
> 2 August 1943, target Hamburg: 16 cans of incendiaries. Flew in electrical storm at 15,000ft for 2hrs, lost 5,000ft. Bad icing. Came out over Sylt. Poor concentration.'

On 16/17 September the crew was part of a force of 340 aircraft which attacked the important railway yards at Modane on the main line from France to Italy:

> We had finished our climb to approximately 15,000ft when the port inner engine burst into flames. I feathered the airscrew, switched off the engine and turned off the master fuel cock and the tank cock, then operated the fire extinguishers. The flames were flaring back over the wing, inside that part of the wing was a main fuel tank. The skipper told

us to put on our parachutes and open the escape hatches. Fortunately the flames began to die down and we returned to our positions.

The remaining three engines were stepped up to climbing power but we were still losing height so the skipper ordered the bomb aimer to drop a 1,000lb bomb (safe, of course) which the navigator plotted on his charts. Finally we managed to hold 11,000ft; some of those mountain peaks looked awfully close.

We reached the target and once the load was gone we were able to climb and cut back the power for more economical cruising. I checked the fuel state and we decided to head for home although we were going to be in trouble if the weather closed down at base and we were given a diversion. The nav had done a preliminary check on a course for Spain if the fuel was not sufficient to get us home.

We came down to approximately 4,000ft after crossing the Alps which enabled us to put the superchargers into 'M' gear which was a saving on power; also, with the air being more dense, it gave us more power for less throttle. The skipper did a super job flying on three engines and we arrived home rather late without too much fuel to spare. The skipper was awarded the DFC soon after this trip.

Returning from ops to Hanover on 27/28 September 1943, W-Willy was caught in heavy flak, although no noticeable damage was sustained.

As the skipper eased W-Willy down on to Mepal's runway at the end of its 14th op, the aircraft seemed to fall to pieces around them.

Later that morning, the maintenance unit crew arrived to take away the pieces and Willy was declared a write-off, but not before the ground-crew sergeant had managed to snatch this photograph of him, battered and bent.

C. DICKENSON

Brief
Lives

Lew Parsons had trained as a flight engineer and arrived with his new crew at Mepal on Saturday 22 August 1943 to join No 75 (New Zealand) Squadron in the opening stages of what became known as the Battle of Berlin. At that time, morale on the squadron was high, but so, too, was fatigue among the aircrews: in the nine days on the squadron before they were shot down, Lew Parsons' crew – skippered by a 'Kiwi' flight sergeant named Doug Henley – had flown 25hrs test-flying and 50hrs operational flying to Berlin (23 August), Friesian Islands and Bordeaux minelaying (24 and 26 August), Nuremberg (27 August) and München Gladbach (30 August). Two

Stirlings of No 90 Squadron lined up at Wratting Common prior to the Berlin raid of 31 August 1943. Of the 106 Stirlings despatched that night, seventeen failed to return. One belonged to No 90 Squadron. *IWM CH10902*

maximum effort raids were flown within 24hrs when, on 31 August, they flew Stirling III EE878:P to Berlin. Many crews were very tired, having had little in the way of sleep since the previous night's raid against München Gladbach. As part of a 613–strong force, Doug Henley's crew took off from Mepal at 20.20hrs on their second trip to 'the Big City':

Berlin's flak and searchlight defences were strong. On approaching the target there appeared to be a wide band of shell-bursts. On entering the area it became apparent that they were in fact at various altitudes and spaced apart. The effect of near misses could be felt as bumps but in the main the approach was more frightening than the close encounter, as long as it wasn't too close.

Searchlights were very menacing but equally or even more hazardous were the chandelier flares dropped along the bombing run and hanging on parachutes for the benefit of the fighters lurking above. Stirling crews felt everything was above – fighters, Lancasters, Halifaxes, etc – except for the fires, TIs and bomb bursts, of course, that helped to silhouette them.

On the occasion that we were attacked we were flying over Berlin on the night of 31 August 1943 and were on our bombing run at about 14,000ft. We had dropped the bombs and the skipper was holding her straight and level to get a good picture when our photoflash exploded. (We had been congratulated after the Nuremberg raid on 27 August for bringing back the best photograph of the target taken by any aircraft from No 3 Group.) At precisely that moment the rear gunner called out 'Weave, skipper, weave, fighter dead astern.'

The pilot threw the aircraft into a dive to port but at the same time cannon shells started striking the aircraft. Our mid-upper gunner Doug Box and the rear gunner Jimmy Grant returned the fire and it seemed to me that all hell had been turned loose. Later, from discussion with the gunners, it became evident that we were attacked by three enemy aircraft, probably Ju88s. Both gunners were sure that at least one of the attackers was destroyed.

When the attack stopped we levelled off and flew away from the target, maintaining the scheduled route for that night (southwest from Berlin to a point between Frankfurt and Cologne, before turning due west to cross Holland and northern France) to avoid being singled out away from the Main Force. Assessing the damage we found our rear gunner was injured in the foot and face and trapped in his turret with the hydraulic operating gear shot away. The mid-upper gunner was concussed in his turret and lying across his guns. Damage to the aircraft was severe with the port inner engine not operating, the tailplane and elevators badly damaged on the port side and holes along the fuselage.

I feathered the port inner engine propeller and shut the fuel cocks, then Bob Quelch (the wireless operator) and I got the rear gunner out of his turret and sat him by the rear escape hatch at the aft end of the bomb-bay. We did our best to bandage his wounded foot but were not very efficient. We got the mid-upper gunner out of his turret and brought him round and sat him with the rear gunner. The pilot was having great difficulty in flying the aircraft due to the damaged tailplane and the unserviceable engine, and he and Ian Smith, the bomb aimer, were struggling to maintain height while the navigator, Cliff Watson, plotted an emergency route to enable us to leave the main stream and head for the coast to ditch the aircraft in the sea, hoping to be rescued by air/sea rescue boats.

Over the intercom the skipper asked me to get rid of all excess weight to lighten the aircraft so I unbolted armour plating, guns, oxygen bottles, belts of ammunition and anything else that was moveable so that Bob Quelch and I could throw it out of the aircraft. I also jettisoned fuel from the main inboard tank but regrettably all these measures were to no avail. We flew on but gradually lost height. We were at the rear hatch throwing equipment out when the skipper suddenly said over the intercom, 'Bale out, bale out!' Those were the last words of a very brave and dedicated pilot to his crew.

Left: Flg Sgt Lew Parsons finished up as a PoW at Stalag IVB after his No 75 (NZ) Squadron Stirling III, EE878: P crashed in Germany while returning from Berlin on the night of 31 August/ 1 September 1943. Along with the two gunners and wireless operator, he was lucky to survive. The pilot, navigator, and bomb aimer were all killed. No 75 Squadron suffered badly that night, losing three aircraft and crews in addition to EE878. *L. PARSONS*

Right: Killed: Flt Sgt Doug Henley RNZAF, pilot, stayed with his aircraft to the last, and died in the inferno which engulfed EE878 after it had crashed in the hills above the Ahr valley, west of Remagen. *L. PARSONS*

Killed: 33-year-old Plt Off Cliff Watson RNZAF, navigator, from Nelson (left), and Sgt Ian Smith RNZAF, 34-year-old bomb aimer, of Hawke's Bay (right), both perished after their parachutes failed to open properly. *L. PARSONS*

The wireless operator baled out; I indicated to the gunners to follow and I went out through the hatch pulling my ripcord almost as I went. Bob hit the ground and sprained an ankle; I was caught by my parachute in a tree. The aircraft crashed on top of a hill further on and burst into flames.

After releasing myself from my 'chute and the tree I started walking in the dark in what I hoped was a westerly direction, only to be captured after about an hour by German soldiers and armed civilians scouring the hills looking for survivors, and was taken to the village of Ahrbruch in the Ahr valley. I learned next day when we met up after being transported to a Luftwaffe camp in the hills that Doug Box and Jimmy Grant, the gunners, were still in the aircraft when it crashed and broke in half. They survived unhurt by the crash, but in the forward part, Doug Henley the pilot was killed instantly and badly burned. Cliff Watson the navigator and Ian Smith the bomb aimer baled out from the front of the aircraft but the Germans found their bodies with the 'chutes not fully opened.

We survivors were taken to Remagen where we changed trains (with much abuse thrown at us by the civilians on the platform) for transport to the Dulag Luft interrogation centre at Frankfurt am Main. After some time in solitary confinement and question sessions by Luftwaffe officers and a fleet air arm type – who got very upset when I asked him why they had scuttled the *Graf Spee* – we were released into the main transit camp. Soon after we joined others to form groups of about forty men per cattletruck and travelled across Germany for over 36hrs, arriving finally at Stammlager IVB in Muhlberg on the River Elbe. We left Jimmy Grant at Frankfurt to have his wounds attended to and didn't see him again until after the war when he was on his way home to New Zealand.

When we were shot down I lost three very good and brave friends; the skipper, navigator and bomb aimer were all killed, but we survivors are in contact to this day and remember our friends with pride and affection.

Although some 1,396 tons of bombs had rained down over the capital of the Reich, the results were fairly unspectacular. But Bomber Command's losses for the night were higher than average with forty-seven aircraft missing, of which seventeen were Stirlings from a force of 106 despatched. No 75 Squadron fared particularly badly, losing four crews out of the twenty it had despatched – the largest force fielded by any squadron in No 3 Group that night. The missing crews were: Flt Sgt E. Roberts (EE918) crashed 10 km SSE of Höxter; Flt Sgt K. McGregor (EF501) shot down by a nightfighter and crashed at Potsdam; Flt Sgt G. Helm (EH905) hit by bombs over the target and crashed at Ludwigsfelde (near Potsdam); and Flt Sgt D. Henley (EE878). Fatigue may well have contributed to this loss rate on the squadron, together with the high number of early returns recorded which totalled eighty-six aircraft.

Down in the Drink

O n the night of 8/9 October 1943, a mixed Bomber Command main force of 430 Lancasters, Halifaxes and Wellingtons delivered a concentrated and devastating attack on Hanover. To draw the German nightfighter force away from the main effort, ninety-five Stirlings and twenty-four Pathfinder 'heavies' were sent on a diversionary raid against Bremen.

Plt Off Phil Dyson and his No 196 Squadron crew were detailed to fly Stirling III EF494 C-Charlie from their base at Witchford in Cambridgeshire on what they hoped would be the final op of their first tour.

On the Beach: Saturday 9 October 1943 and Phil Dyson with his No 196 Squadron crew (minus one) pose for the camera on the beach at Hemsby, Norfolk, following their successful ditching the night before in Stirling EF494:C.

In the background can be seen the tailfin of C-Charlie, rising above the swell, several hundred yards off the shoreline.

From left to right: Phil Dyson, pilot: Bud Rattigan, WOp/AG; Jack Parker, rear gunner; Dudley Northover, navigator; Peter Hooker, flight engineer; Don Benning, mid-upper gunner.
P. DYSON

At briefing that night a strong emphasis had been placed on the need for navigational accuracy and perfect timing; lone aircraft would be sitting ducks for the Luftwaffe nightfighter crews, so when C-Charlie's take-off was delayed it was an unwelcome complication, as Phil Dyson recalls:

The remains of C-Charlie were a familiar sight at Hemsby for several years after the ditching when they were uncovered during particularly low tides. Eventually, the effects of tidal action – shifting the sand and shingle – buried the wreckage from view. In this photograph taken during the summer of 1946, 5-year-old Lionel Kett finds much of interest in the wrecked fuselage centre-section of C-Charlie. He is standing between the wing spars with the oxygen bottle stowages visible to the left and right. The upper fuselage covering has gone and the interior has filled with sand and pebbles. *G. KETT via P. DYSON*

The pre-flight check which every self-preserving pilot carried out very carefully indeed, revealed that the pilot's escape hatch was unlocked. Combined efforts to move the locking lever over to the 'shut' position failed to secure the latch but, finally, with the assistance of a sergeant fitter, it was declared well and truly locked and C-Charlie roared down the runway three minutes late.

We had gained little more than 50ft in height after take-off when Jack Parker, the rear gunner, remarked that something had just hit the tail and, simultaneously, I announced the loss of the escape hatch when a great gale-force wind blew above my head. With commendable imagination my 19-year-old flight engineer, Peter Hooker, commandeered the navigator's green canvas chart case and within a few minutes, with the skill of a surgeon, he had fixed a canopy above my head which reduced the gale to a fairly stiff breeze.

The decision was made, perhaps unwisely, to proceed on course to Bremen, and increased boost gradually made up for lost time. We approached the Dutch coast and we could see the unseen stream of those in front attracting the attention of the German attack on the Friesian Islands. Troubles rarely come singly they say.

The flight engineer suddenly reported the port inner engine was giving trouble (it was running very hot although that was not an infrequent occurrence), but two minutes later he requested me to cut the offending engine – which I did – and feather the propeller. The spectre of an engine fire constantly haunted aircrews. There was hardly time to consider the prospect of flying over Bremen with three engines when my young engineer somewhat tremulously exclaimed 'Skipper, the port outer, the same bloody thing. We've lost oil pressure and the temperature is way above limit. We've got to feather the port outer.'

There was no argument and C-Charlie swung around on to a reciprocal course pointing homewards and we lightened the load by releasing our 6,000lb bombload. Once the calculations had been made, several hundred gallons of petrol were also jettisoned over the North Sea. C-Charlie gave an almost audible sigh of relief and bravely responded to full trim and full rudder to continue on a course to East Anglia.

We decided to land at Woodbridge where so many American aircraft in distress had successfully landed, but hopes were dashed when Bud Rattigan, our Canadian wireless op, calmly informed us that the whole of East Anglia was enveloped in a thick ground mist. We were left with the alternative of ditching the aircraft.

Coming up to the East Anglian coast we were at 3,000ft and I made a slow turn to run parallel with the shore. It was very dark but the land was more discernible than I thought it would be, and the coast ahead appeared to be long and straight. Ditching was something one could not practise, but learning the ditching procedure was a lesson which each individual crew member took very seriously.

The pilot had to be securely strapped into his seat – and was not, and I could do little for myself for I needed both hands to control the aircraft.

'Norman,' I called to the bomb aimer, who occupied the adjacent seat, 'Fasten my seat belt.' There were four straps which met on a central clip-in device. It was dark and Norman groped around.

Meanwhile, throttle back and reduce speed, one-third flap and, to the wireless op, Bud, who had already sent out distress signals, 'Let the trailing aerial out.' I needed his instant warning when the aerial touched the water at 20ft as the signal to cut the engines, pull back on the control column and stall C-Charlie in tail-first.

We were down to 500ft and Norman was still fumbling around. 'Norman, strap yourself in quickly and hold the strap across my chest.' It seemed no more than seconds after I had throttled right back that C-Charlie hit the water with an immense thud and the impact threw me forward with an almighty bang as my head struck the window in front and we went down.

Momentarily concussed, a flood of cold sea water crashed through the hatch above and instantly revived me, and I jumped onto the seat and squeezed my bulky figure through that small aperture. Miraculously, C-Charlie was afloat and I could see my friends climbing out of the mid-upper gun escape hatch one by one, all except one. We found Norman Luff, the bomb aimer, entangled with the control column and we freed him and dragged him out of the pilot's escape hatch.

Down by the port wing the dinghy was there and waiting, fully inflated, and we gingerly clambered down, fearful lest we put our feet through the base. Pete, the flight engineer, cut the lanyard and Jack and Bud inexpertly paddled us towards the shore where we could see a light and hear a voice shouting repeatedly 'Steer this way, straight toward the light.' In a few minutes we entered the surf and stepped ashore where the voice continued, 'Now, one behind the other and follow me,' and we crunched our way up a steep shingled beach.

At the top we could hear female voices and they led us towards a large house where we took off our soaking uniforms and flying kit and wrapped ourselves in a variety of garments. They tendered first aid to Norman who had a deep gash in his leg, they fed us and eventually provided us with beds for the few hours left before dawn. These angels were members of the Women's Royal Naval Auxiliary and 'manned' a listening post where they had heard our Mayday call, never dreaming we would drop in to visit them at Hemsby, which lies some 10 miles north of Great Yarmouth, Norfolk.

In the early hours of the morning I slipped out of the house and saw the huge tail of the Stirling, standing like a sentinel, some 300yds off shore. Later we all lined up with several of our hostesses to have our photographs taken with our staunch friend C-Charlie in the background. We had been very lucky in a number of ways, not least in the fact that we had landed just off a mined beach!

Phil Dyson, Peter Hooker, Bud Rattigan and Jack Parker all lived to fight another day and ultimately survived the perils and dangers of wartime flying. But for the other three crew members, the sweet fruits of peace which they had all fought so hard to win were not destined to be theirs to enjoy.

Commissioned and awarded the DFC, Phil Dyson's close friend Dudley Northover, the navigator, enlisted for a further tour of ops with No 149 Squadron – still on Stirlings – and was killed in action over southern France on a Special Duties operation on 11 April 1944.

Norman Luff, the bomb aimer, and Don Benning, the mid-upper gunner, both flew further tours with No 196 Squadron in its new role as an airborne squadron in No 38 Group. Norman Luff and his crew disappeared without trace

Some twenty-five years later, in November 1971, tidal action uncovered the badly corroded remains of C-Charlie. Here can be seen the port outer engine bay, wing trailing edge and the attachment point for the aileron (left), and one of the huge main undercarriage assemblies (below) on the shore at Hemsby.

The remains of C-Charlie were cleared to prevent them from causing a hazard to local fishermen. Preservation, however desirable, would have been very difficult bearing in mind the badly corroded state of C-Charlie. *P. DYSON*

on 6 June 1944, taking part in the airborne assault on the River Orne and Caen Canal. His aircraft was probably shot down by flak and crashed in the English Channel.

Don Benning and his crew took part in the ill-fated Operation 'Market Garden', and he was killed in a resupply drop to the beleaguered 1st Airborne Division at Arnhem on 20 September 1944. His Stirling was one of eleven shot down on that day alone.

After all that they had been through together, the hand of fate might have been expected to show some compassion towards them. But the Grim Reaper was, if nothing else, totally arbitrary in his choice of those whom he took away to Valhalla.

STIRLING AIRCRAFT – DINGHY DRILL

PILOT

'Dinghy, Dinghy! Prepare for ditching.'

1. Takes off chute harness if possible and ensures Sutton Harness is secure. Keeps crew informed of aircraft situation right up until time of warning for impact. Jettisons top escape hatch when ready. Lowers landing light.
2. Ditching stations at controls.
3. 'Ditched OK. Outside, chaps.' Leaves by F1.

NAVIGATOR

Acknowledge 5

1. Releases B/A, checks security of front parachute exit. Returns to table, gives W/Op DR position and course. Gives pilot estimated surface windspeed and direction. Collects pyros, pistols, etc, and places in navigation bag. Proceeds to ditching station with bag when ordered by pilot. Closes armoured door.
2. Lying on floor, starboard side, with legs against armoured door, hands clasped behind head. On intercom.

3. Hands navigation bag to W/Op. Leaves M2 and makes way to dinghy. Stands by to release it manually from wing if necessary.

BOMB AIMER

Acknowledge 6

1. Vacates turret and closes doors. Puts bombs safe. Puts out ⅓rd flap and fixes pilot's Sutton Harness. Jettisons bombs and ensures bomb doors closed again. Assists pilot generally. 'K' dinghy on 2nd pilot's seat. Removes astro hatch, takes up ditching station and informs pilot.
2. Sitting on floor, back against rear of rear spar, starboard side, braces with hands clasped behind head. Intercom to rest position.
3. Leaves R2 and makes way to dinghy with radio.

FLIGHT ENGINEER

Acknowledge 4

1. Calculates remaining flying time on petrol. Removes astrodome platform. Stands by for manual operation of bomb doors, flaps, and petrol jettison if necessary. Proceeds to

ditching station when ordered by pilot. Informs pilot when R/G and MU/G are in position and keeps them supplied with all gen from pilot.

2. Sitting on floor, back against rear of rear spar, port side, braced with hands clasped behind head. Intercom to position of port side between spars.

3. Pulls internal dinghy release. Leaves R4, grasps painter and controls dinghy until all are aboard.

WIRELESS OPERATOR
Acknowledge 3

1. Commences distress signals procedure in co-operation with navigator (course, height and ground speed, estimated position of ditching) and continues until ordered to ditching station by navigator. Clamps down Morse key and changes to fixed aerial.

2. Lying on floor, port side with legs braced against armoured door, hands clasped behind head. On intercom.

3. Leaves M1 and makes way to dinghy with navigation bag.

MID-UPPER GUNNER
Acknowledge 2

1. Vacates turret, opens and secures mid-top hatch, fixes ladder in position. Tears off cover from external dinghy release point. Takes up ditching position.

2. Lying on floor port side with legs braced against draught-proof door, hands clasped behind head.

3. Hands dinghy radio and any equipment to B/A outside. Leaves R3.

REAR GUNNER
Acknowledge 1

1. Vacates turret and closes doors. Checks security of rear parachute exit and main door. Proceeds with axe to ditching station, ensures dinghy radio and aerial mast are close at hand.

2. Lying on floor, starboard side with legs braced against draught-proof door, hands clasped behind head.

3. Leaves R1 and pulls external dinghy release. Stands by to release dinghy manually from wing if necessary.

KEY TO ABBREVIATIONS:
1. Initial action on 'prepare for ditching' order
2. Crew member moves to his appropriate ditching station
3. Post-ditching action and duties

POINTS OF EXIT:
F = Pilot's escape hatch (pilot)
M = Astrodome (wireless operator, navigator)
R = Mid-top escape hatch (rear gunner, bomb aimer, mid-upper gunner, flight engineer)

The Fear Within

After leaving Harold Street School in Cleethorpes at the age of 14, Bob Grant became apprenticed to his uncle – also Bob – as a compositor in the family printing business. But hot metal was not enough and the urge to learn to fly got the better of him and a friend, Jim Short.

In March 1939, at the age of 23, Bob enlisted in the RAF and was put on reserve until he began his pilot training in May 1940. On gaining his wings he passed to No 15 OTU at Harwell before joining his first front-line squadron,

WO Bob Grant (standing, third from left) of No 218 (Gold Coast) Squadron. A more deserving recipient of the DFC would have been hard to find. By the time he had been screened from ops in February 1944 after his second tour, he had flown a grand total of 1,277hrs 25mins since joining up in 1940. *S. GRANT*

No 9, at Honington on New Year's Day 1941. He flew Wellingtons on ops until posted overseas with No 70 Squadron in May to Kabrit in the Western Desert. Bob completed a tour on Wellingtons, returning home in January 1942 to instruct on No 1665 HCU and No 12 OTU. In July 1943, realising that he probably stood a greater chance of survival on ops than teaching inexperienced boys to fly clapped-out Wimpys, he converted to Stirlings at Woolfox Lodge with No 1665 HCU and as a warrant officer pilot joined No 218 Squadron at Downham Market on 7 August 1943.

Bob's second tour opened on 10 August with a 7hr trip to Nuremberg in Stirling III MZ263; he and his crew flew seven more trips until they had three early returns in September:

> Forgetting the pisspot was the trigger for my morale drop. The tin was always carried on ops for those calls of nature but on one occasion we forgot it and we turned back. We had been briefed to attack Hanover on 22 September but after take-off I couldn't get the airspeed up and we fell way behind the stream. As we reached the Dutch coast my nerve failed me; I just couldn't face it so we turned back. We turned back on the following night en route to Mannheim, and on the 27th against Hanover again.

Bob and his crew find time for a spot of skylarking at Downham Market in the autumn of 1943. From left to right: Sgt H. Bossick, flight engineer; WO Bob Grant, pilot; Sgt L. Clay, rear gunner; Flt Sgt G. Sivell, wireless operator; Flg Off Tommy Thomas, navigator; Sgt Freddie Lambert, mid-upper gunner. S. GRANT

Stirlings of No 218 Squadron in their element, up above the clouds. The squadron equipped with the Mk I at Marham in December 1941 and flew its final operation with the Mk III from Downham Market on 2 August 1944. *A. LONG via JR/SBRL*

Bombs Gone! A Stirling bomb aimer at his station in the nose of the aircraft. IWM CH3293

Bob and his crew were checked out by their flight commander on 28 September and declared fit for operations. They flew seven more ops during October and early November: Kassel and Frankfurt on the 3rd and 4th; a 'gardening' (mine-laying) sortie on the 7th; Bremen on the 8th; more 'gardening' on 4 November, then to Ludwigshafen on the 18th. His nerve was beginning to come back.

On 22 November the Stirling crews of No 218 Squadron were briefed to bomb Berlin. The weather forecast was good with fairly clear weather over bases in England, although the greater part of Germany would be covered in low cloud and fog. Maximum effort was ordered and 764 aircraft took to the air, of which fifty were Stirlings. The raid was to be concentrated in five waves with the most experienced crews in the van and the new ones bringing up the rear. This meant that the Stirlings, which were normally allotted their own exclusive wave, were in some danger of being bombed from above.

This is the view from over Düsseldorf on 10/11 September 1942, as experienced by a bomb aimer. Broad fire tracks and smoke obscure the view.
IWM CH3128

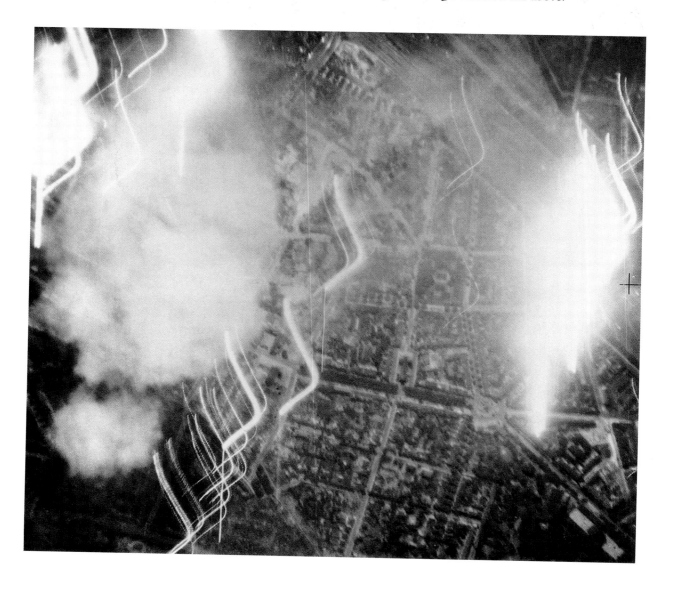

However, the weather deteriorated rapidly with 10/10 cloud and icing conditions, bad enough even to ground most Luftwaffe nightfighters. Bob and his crew took off in Stirling III EH942:M at 1700hrs:

> There was widespread fog at our base and it wasn't until we had climbed above 10,000ft that we broke out of the cloud. I put the kite's nose down on the run-in to the target with our airspeed building to 200 IAS at 7,000ft. We were way below the Main Force and the flak barrage. We dropped our load and made for home, arriving back at base at midnight.

This succinct and self-effacing account of one night in the life of WO Bob Grant belies the true reality of events. For his part in the Berlin raid of 22/23 November Bob was awarded a well-deserved DFC. The impartial wording of the official citation says it all:

> Warrant Officer Grant has participated in numerous sorties, throughout which he has displayed a high degree of courage and determination.
>
> In November 1943, while participating in a sortie against Berlin, very bad weather and ice conditions were encountered, but owing to his initiative and skill the target was located and a successful attack delivered from a low altitude.
>
> Warrant Officer Grant's enthusiasm and devotion to duty have evoked the confidence of all with whom he has flown.

Plt Off G.L. Jenkins DFC and his crew were transferred from No 218 Squadron on 12 August to form the new No 623 Squadron. They were shot down over Nuremberg on 28 August in Stirling III EE909:H by the dual action of a nightfighter and a Halifax. Plt Off Jenkins, the skipper, was killed and the rest of the crew became PoWs. They are pictured here during July 1943 with a tally board for the Stirlings bearing the call sign H-Harry which had served with the squadron up to that time. From left to right: Sgt J. Schofield, flight engineer; Sgt V. Hawkins, mid-upper gunner; Sgt Dickerson, wireless operator; Sgt R. Booth, rear gunner; Plt Off G. Jenkins, pilot; Plt Off Ted Pierce, navigator; Plt Off Shaw, bomb aimer. *E. PIERCE via JR/SBRL*

OFFICE USE ONLY.

47/1937
1:100,000.
10/39.

Lat: 53° 05'N.
Long: 8° 47'E.
Alt: 8 ft.
Circles: 1 mile.
Scale: 1:63,360.

NOTES.
Spot levels are shown in metres.
The brown marking on map indicates the
direction of main roads.
HOSPITALS ARE MARKED ⊕ AND MUST BE AVOIDED

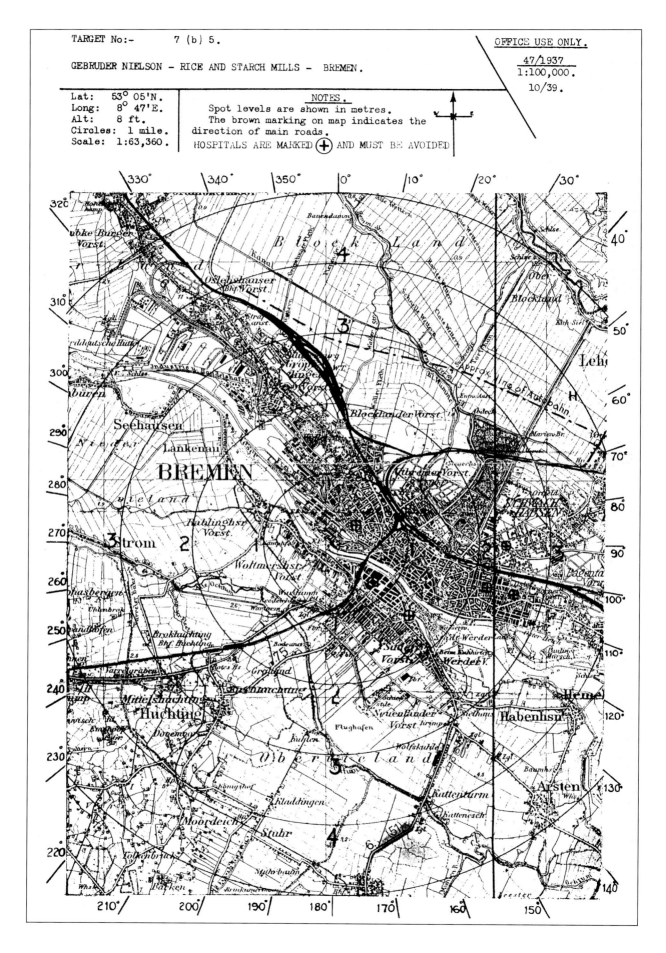

Not only had Bob fought and won battles over the cities of the Reich, but he had also conquered the insidious enemy that lurked in his mind – fear. A more deserving candidate for the DFC would have been difficult to find.

Bob flew a further five ops, completing his second tour in February 1944 and was screened from ops. He instructed with Nos 1653 HCU and 105 OTU before joining No 167 Squadron, Transport Command, shortly after the war's end, flying Wellingtons and Warwicks on freight runs until his demob in July 1946.

The raid of 22/23 November was the first real success for Harris in the Battle of Berlin, with some 2,501 tons of bombs going down over the Big City for the loss of twenty-six aircraft, of which five were Stirlings. Nine crews had been briefed from No 218 Squadron, of which five returned early, three attacked the primary target and one skippered by Sqn Ldr G.W. Prior DFC crashed in the target area.

As part of the broader canvas of events, of the fifty Stirlings despatched that night, twelve had returned early and five had been lost. In the three raids of the Battle of Berlin so far, 280 Stirling sorties had been flown, forty-six had made early returns and thirty-seven had been lost, which represented a casualty rate of 13.2 per cent of those despatched, and 15.2 per cent of those which had reached the shores of occupied Europe.

Bob Grant's crew flew their twelfth op to Bremen in Stirling III EH942 on 8 October 1943. The large-scale (1:63,360) map reproduced here was used by Flg Off Tommy Thomas on this trip and is typical of many of this scale used by Bomber Command's navigators for detailed target identification during the Second World War. *via S. GRANT*

For
Valour

The Second World War saw many acts of heroism by members of the Commonwealth air forces, played out against the backdrop of a blazing bomber cockpit or struggling through a veil of pain and exhaustion to bring a badly crippled aircraft home to safety. Among these, two Stirling pilots became recipients of the British Commonwealth's highest award for valour, the Victoria Cross. Both men were NCOs and were posthumously awarded the VC for their bravery on long range operations to Italy. There are surely also many other instances of bravery and sacrifice in the air which we shall never know about, because no one survived to tell the tale.

Flt Sgt Ron Middleton RAAF of No 149 Squadron was very seriously injured by flak over Turin on 28 November 1942 and managed to fly his badly

damaged aircraft home. Running short of fuel and likely to crash at any moment, he gave his crew the order to bale out at Dymchurch, Kent, before turning the Stirling out to sea to avoid crashing on any centres of population. Four of his crew managed to bale out successfully, but the flight engineer and nose turret gunner delayed, perishing when they jumped into the icy sea. Middleton stayed with his aircraft to the last, both diving into the sea in the small hours of 29 November, several miles off the coast near Dymchurch.

The bodies of Sgt John Mackie, the gunner, and Sgt Jimmy Jeffery, the flight engineer,

Flt Sgt Ron Middleton VC,
No 149 Squadron, RAF.
IWM CH8165

Flt Sgt Arthur Aaron VC,
No 218 Squadron, RAF. *IWM*

were recovered from the sea the following day, but it was not until 1 February 1943 that Ron Middleton's body was found, washed up on the Kent coast by the tide.

Arthur Aaron, a 21-year-old Yorkshireman from Leeds, was the other Stirling pilot to receive the VC for his leadership and superhuman endurance, despite horrific wounds which eventually claimed his young life.

The author is indebted to Alistair McFarlane for permission to use the following account, which he wrote after hearing at first-hand a description of the events of 12 August 1943 from Jim Richmond of Selby, Yorkshire, mid-upper gunner in Flt Sgt Arthur Aaron's No 218 Squadron crew.

At 14.40hrs on 12 August 1943, Flt Sgt Arthur Aaron took his crew and aircraft on a low-flying air-test lasting 50mins. Little did they know then what would happen on the op that night to Turin.

They left Downham Market at 21.30hrs in Stirling III EF452 en route to Italy and were cruising normally over the Alps as Aaron gradually descended to 9,000ft to commence his bombing run.

Malcolm Mitchem, the flight engineer, came forward from his panel in the fuselage and sat on Aaron's right in the second pilot's seat. Allan Larden, the Canadian bomb aimer, went down into the nose compartment to operate the bomb-sight. Bill Brennan, the navigator, carried on with his job of working out their return course. Jimmy Guy, at 35 years the oldest member of the crew, made his way under the mid-upper turret to the rear fuselage to ensure the photoflash fell when the bombs dropped. The two gunners, Richmond at mid-upper and McCabe in the rear, kept a look-out for fighters.

Jim Richmond spotted another Stirling making a weaving approach to the target on their right and he called to Aaron, 'Watch that bloke up front, Art.' 'I've got him,' Aaron replied, asking for bomb doors open at the same time.

Mitchem leaned forward to operate the lever and noticed that the other Stirling was now no more than 250yds away. Suddenly the intercom was alive with shouts as the rear gunner from the other aircraft raked them from wingtip to wingtip with machine-gun fire.

In the cockpit, the windscreen shattered on Aaron's side and a hail of flying perspex covered everyone. Mitchem felt a blow on his ankle but was otherwise unharmed.

The aircraft slewed to the left and dived away, the airspeed rapidly building up. Mitchem's concern for his engines made him start for his instrument panel, but as the moonlight flooded the cockpit he saw Aaron's face: he had been hit in the lower jaw and lost his oxygen mask and microphone which made it look to Mitchem as though half his face

Sgt Arthur Aaron (right) on his arrival at No 1657 HCU at Stradishall in March 1943. With him are Sgt Tom McCabe, rear gunner (left), and Sgt Bill Brennan, navigator. *A. LONG via JR/SBRL*

had been shot away. His right arm was almost severed at the elbow and he had severe chest wounds. Yet, he remained conscious as Mitchem grabbed the controls and pulled back as hard as he could, levelling the Stirling out at about 3,000ft.

Whilst this was happening, the others were taking stock of their situation. Brennan, the navigator, had been killed by a single bullet through the heart, and lay in a crumpled heap over his bloodstained charts. The throttle control pedestal was wrecked, and two of the throttle controls shot away completely. The starboard outer was losing power and the only engine controllable was the port outer.

Larden and Guy dragged Aaron from his seat and back into the fuselage to make him more comfortable. Then Larden went forward to take over the controls, sitting in Aaron's seat to help Mitchem. Unaware that their bomb load had hung up, they desperately tried to gain height out of the maze of valleys around them. Increasing the revs on the good engine, the aircraft slowly started a crabbed climb to the right to clear the mountainous landscape. At last they were clear and saw a wide expanse of sea stretching out before them.

They had no idea where they were or where to go, so Larden and Guy went to the navigator's table to discuss their position. They worked out that they were off La Spezia, on the coast of northern Italy. Deciding to head for Sicily, they then discovered that the charts did not extend that far south. Larden, therefore, drew a blob to represent Sicily and took the result forward to agree a course with Mitchem. Guy suggested that they fly south until he could get a bearing from Bone airfield in North Africa. He had already sent a message back to base informing them of their plight, but he had received no answer. He had little success with Malta or Bone, either. Both appeared to be in contact with the aircraft but, as they were using different codes, neither could understand any message.

It was decided to call Bone in plain language. Although strictly against orders, their plight was desperate. This worked and they were able to plot that they had at least another 400 miles to fly before reaching Bone. In the meantime Aaron had recovered sufficiently to take an interest in what was happening. Because of the shattered windscreen the noise in the aircraft was deafening, and Guy wrote a note for him to say they were heading for North Africa.

For more than two hours they flew on. Jim Richmond shared the strain of flying the bomber, which was constantly on stalling point and had to be flown in 20min spells in order to rest from the exhausting business of hanging on to the controls.

At last they saw a pyramid of light on the horizon. The searchlights at Bone had been used to provide a guiding beacon for the crippled aircraft. After a short discussion the crew decided to crash-land the Stirling on its belly, blissfully unaware that the bomb load was still on board.

Whilst circling to lose height before the final approach, Aaron signalled to Guy to ask what was happening. Still unable to speak, he struggled to rise from the floor. He could barely move but he motioned to Guy that he wanted to be up front. Mitchem got out of the left-hand seat and went back to help Guy and the two gunners lift Aaron forward. They struggled to put him in his seat, but nobody would think to stop him. Indeed, his very presence in his rightful place was a tremendous psychological boost to them all.

With his left hand he began the approach, indicating with movements of his head while the rest of the crew took up their crash positions. Dissatisfied with the approach, Aaron took the aircraft round again. Once more they tried, but still Aaron did not feel that it was right. Mitchem, who knew to the last drop how far their fuel had gone, felt certain that their next approach had to be their last.

On the next circuit Mitchem stood behind Aaron. At 20–30ft above the ground, Aaron again began to pull back on the stick. 'Go down, go down!' screamed Larden, 'There's not enough petrol for another circuit!' In desperation, he leaned across and pushed Aaron from the control column, who collapsed in his seat and gave Larden a look he would never forget.

The Stirling was now falling from 100ft and Larden pushed the control column forward. There was a solid thump and the aircraft was down, scraping along the earth in a choking cloud of dust.

When motionless, they evacuated the aircraft and removed the bodies of Aaron and the dead navigator. Aaron was taken away in an ambulance, but there was nothing they could do. Nine hours later

The surviving members of Arthur Aaron's crew pictured at Bone airfield in North Africa during August 1943. They returned to the UK on 14 September. From left to right: Tom McCabe, rear gunner; Jim Richmond, mid-upper gunner; Allan Larden, bomb aimer; Malcolm Mitchem, flight engineer; Jimmy Guy, wireless operator. *IWM CHA1228*

he passed away. Had he been content to give in and lie in the fuse lage, medical opinion was that despite his terrible injuries he might have lived.

On 14 December 1943, Arthur Louis Aaron was postumously awarded the Victoria Cross, the citation stating:

Nine hours after landing, Flt Sgt Aaron died from exhaustion. Had he been content, when grievously wounded, to lie still and conserve his failing strength, he would probably have recovered. But he saw it as his duty to exert himself to the utmost, if necessary with his last breath, to ensure that his aircraft and his crew did not fall into enemy hands. In appalling conditions he showed the greatest qualities of courage, determination and leadership and though wounded and dying he set an example of devotion to duty which has seldom been equalled and never surpassed.

The page from Jim Richmond's logbook which records the events of 12 August 1943, resulting in the award of a posthumous VC to his skipper.

J. RICHMOND via A. MCFARLANE

"B" FLIGHT 218 SQUADRON

DOWNHAM MARKET

Time carried forward :— 83.30. 90.50.

Date	Hour	Aircraft Type and No.	Pilot	Duty	Remarks (including results of bombing, gunnery, exercises, etc.)	Flying Times Day	Flying Times Night
Aug. 1st	15.20	EF-452	Sgt. Aaron	a/g.	air test	1-00	
" 2nd	23.45	EF.452	Sgt. Aaron	a/g.	15. OPS: HAMBURG – D.N.C.O		4-15
" 12	14.40	EF.452	"	a/g.	air test + low flying	·50	
" 12th	21.30	EF.452	"	"	16. OPS TURIN. SHOT up by A/C. Navigator killed. Pilot died of wounds. B/A + F/Engr. wounded. Crash landed in North Africa Bone aerodrome.		8.40
						85-20	95-05

S/L
O.C. 'B' FLIGHT - 218 SQUADRON

W/CDR
O.C. 218 (GOLD COAST) SQUADRON

Summary for August.
'B' FLIGHT. 1943
Hrs flown day 1.50
Hrs flown night 12.55.
TOTAL FLYING HRS. 14.45

PILOT. DIED NINE. HOURS. AFTER WE LANDED.

James Richmond

TOTAL TIME ... 85·20 95·05
103·45

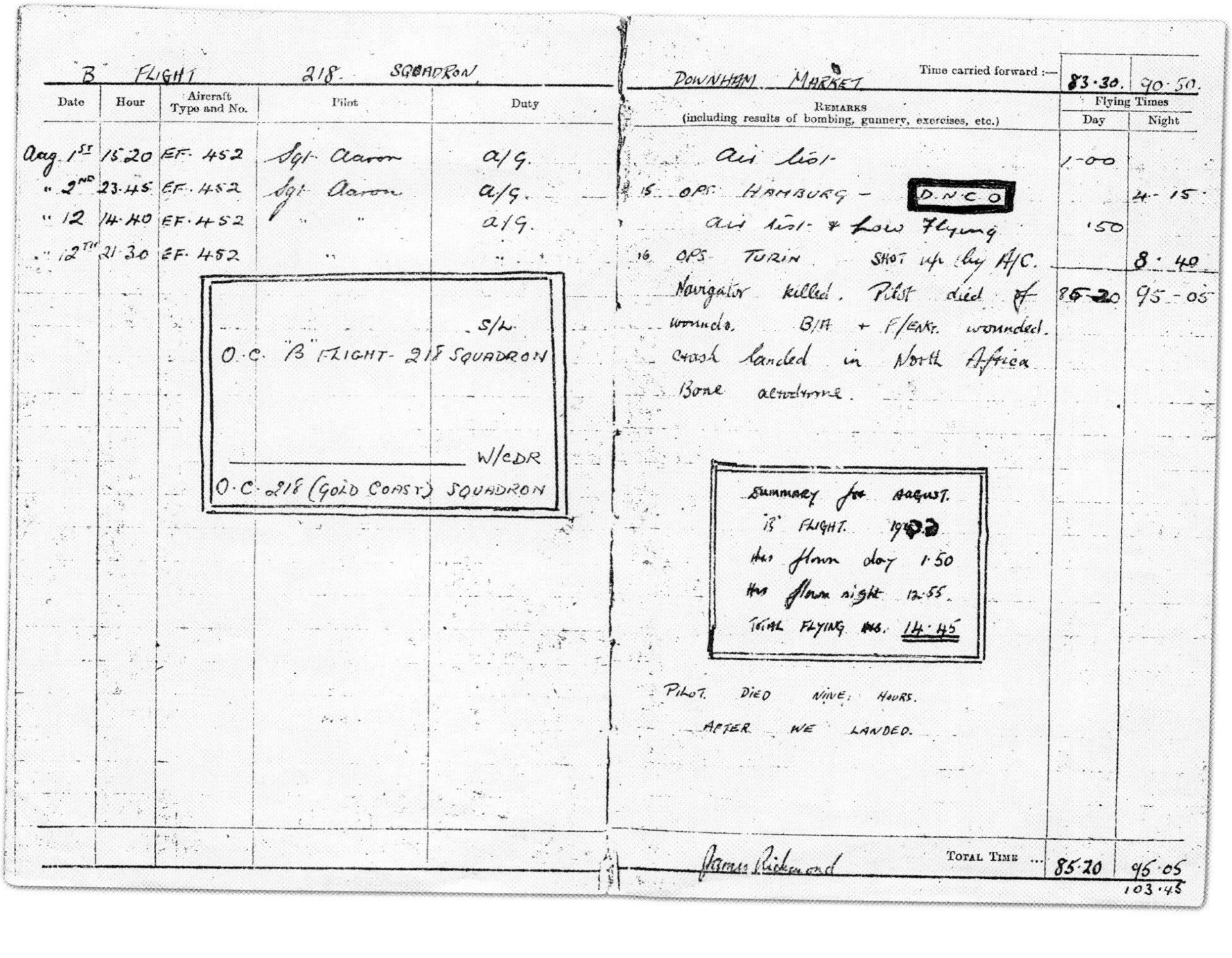

Allan Larden was awarded the Conspicuous Gallantry Medal, and the DFM went to Mitchem and Guy. The two gunners, Richmond and McCabe, received nothing – the squadron gunnery leader who would have recommended them was killed in action during their absence and their names were never put forward.

Since the true account of the incident would have been bad for morale, the authorities encouraged the media to speculate that enemy action was responsible. Some held the gunners responsible for failing to spot the 'enemy' aircraft! However, behind the scenes the RAF had examined the other 100 or so navigational logs and charts of the other Stirling crews who had flown that night, establishing beyond doubt the identity of the other Stirling by pinpointing the position of the two aircraft at the time of the incident. What action was taken against the rear gunner of the other aircraft was not disclosed, and probably never will be.

Jim Richmond was screened from ops and posted to No 17 OTU on 11 October 1943 as a gunnery instructor.

Gardening

On 25 March 1942 Bomber Command assumed overall responsibility from Coastal Command for airborne mining operations in home waters as part of the campaign against German sea traffic. Although the Admiralty was responsible for all sea mining, whether or not it was carried out by aircraft, naval surface craft or submarine, the operational aspects of sea mining by aircraft were carried out by Bomber Command. Naval Staff Officers were attached to all Bomber Group headquarters for the purpose of briefing group and station intelligence officers on the requirements for mine-laying, while at station level, Royal Navy petty officers advised RAF armourers in the preparation of mines.

Mining operations were codenamed 'gardening', and the mines themselves referred to as 'vegetables'. Bomber Command planted its vegetables in some eighty gardens with such charming names as 'Lettuce' (the Kiel Canal), 'Silverthorn' (the Kattegat), and 'Broccoli' and 'Asparagus' (areas off the Danish Great Belt).

Favourite and fruitful plots for gardening activities included the Norway/Baltic sea passage through the Kattegat, the approaches to the Atlantic U-boat bases, and rivers and estuaries through which passed a variety of enemy sea traffic. Additionally, the sea lanes off the coasts of northern Germany, Denmark, Holland, France and the Bay of Biscay proved profitable areas in which to sow mines.

The main objective of airborne sea mining operations was to plant the mines in the enemy's narrow swept channels and waterways from heights that varied from as low as a few hundred feet to 12,000ft. At the lower heights mining was extremely dangerous for aircrews who were prey to light flak and small arms fire from shore and ship-borne defences. By the end of 1943, experiments had

Armourers prepare 1,500lb A Mk I-IV aerial mines in the bomb dump at North Creake prior to despatch to No 199 Squadron's Stirlings waiting at dispersal. Along with the smaller 1,000lb A Mk V, the A Mk I-IV was the aerial mine most widely used during the Second World War by the RAF and incorporated a number of triggering devices which included magnetic, acoustic or a combination of both. Approximately half the mine's weight was taken up by high explosive Amatol or Minol.
During 1944, some 17,493 mines were planted from the air in coastal waters stretching from the Baltic to the Bay of Biscay.
199 REGISTER via JR/SBRL

been made in mine-laying from greater heights with the use of H2S, although dropping mines with the assistance of the radio aid Gee was generally forbidden because of its inherent east-west or north-south error. However, Gee was useful for navigating to a suitable visual pin-point from which to make a timed run to drop mines. With ground speeds of 180–200mph and runs of about 12 miles, mines were dropped with intervals of about three seconds between each, and crews were instructed to maintain the same straight and level course for 2–3mins after the drop to further confuse the enemy as to the precise dropping zone.

Although the first operational use of converted sea mines had been made on 12/13 August 1940 by Hampdens of Nos 49 and 83 Squadrons, the Stirling was not to become involved in mine-laying for another 18 months. Mines were delivered to Oakington in early 1941 but it was not until 23 March 1942 that three crews of No XV Squadron carried out the first 'gardening' sorties by Stirlings off the coast of Brittany between Lorient and the Ile de Groix. On the following night three crews from No 149 Squadron planted twelve mines in the same area.

Initially, the Stirling was capable of carrying only four mines, but after modifications to its fuselage bomb doors six could be carried, enabling it to compete on equal terms with the Lancaster – at least when it came to 'gardening'. Of the other types used for the task, the Manchester and Halifax could each carry four mines, while the Wellington could manage only two.

Mining sorties increased during 1943 with some 550 mines sown in March alone, although this success was not without its price in blood. On 28/29 April that year a mixed force of 167 aircraft laid 593 mines off Heligoland, in the River Elbe and in the Great and Little Belts. Twenty-five Stirlings from Nos 75, 90, 214 and 218 Squadrons mined the Belts area at low level, where flak ships and nightfighters claimed eight of them. A further five aircraft from the force were lost in the most costly mine-laying operation of the war. Stirlings continued operating in the 'gardening' role until late in July 1944 when

Flt Lt G. Newsome (left) poses with an unidentified aircrew beside EH930:N at Lakenheath in early 1944. Originally delivered to No 75 Squadron on 20 July 1943, the aircraft was transferred to No XV Squadron on 28 July the same year, coded LS-A, completing nineteen ops before passing to No 199 Squadron on 27 December and flying a further sixteen ops. On 12 May 1944 she was transferred to No 1651 HCU before being SOC on 24 April 1945.

LANCE SMITH via JR/SBRL

One for the folks back home: in this posed photograph of a 'gather-up' crew taken at Mepal after an air test in early 1944 for a New Zealand newspaper, only two members of Jim Murray's No 75 (NZ) Squadron crew are featured.

Flg Off Jim Murray, in the doorway, helps Flt Sgt John McFarland to climb the crew ladder. At the far right is Flt Sgt Alan Bromley, a WOp/AG, also fated not to survive the war. Flying on ops to Dortmund in No 75 Squadron's Lancaster ME690, skippered by Plt Off Laurence Burke on 22/23 May the same year, his aircraft was shot down near Louvain, Belgium. There were no survivors.

Stirling III EF181 was equally unfortunate after it was transferred to No 218 (Gold Coast) Squadron in March. On 12 June it burst a tyre on take-off, swung, broke its starboard undercarriage leg and subsequently was written off.

J.L. MCFARLAND

No 199 Squadron's Stirling III EH930:N undergoes a final engine run-up before taking off from Lakenheath on a mine-laying operation in the spring of 1944. *IWM CH12683*

Sgt Hiram Kahler, the 21-year-old flight engineer in Flg Off Jim Murray's No 75 Squadron crew, was one of four crew killed when Stirling EH955:K was shot down by a nightfighter over Denmark on 18 April 1944.

MRS MIRIAM COHEN

No 218 Squadron flew the type's final mine-laying sortie to the Brest area on the 23rd.

No 75 (New Zealand) Squadron based at Mepal in Cambridgeshire had flown Stirlings on 210 sorties since November 1942, of which 107 had been mine-laying. At the beginning of April the squadron took delivery of its first Lancasters and by the 26th it had relinquished its last Stirling.

A few weeks before they were shot down by a nightfighter on 18 April 1944, navigator John 'Paddy' McFarland's No 75 Squadron crew had converted from Stirlings on to Lancasters and had actually flown several ops on the Lanc. The reason for reverting to a Stirling for the 'last op' was a volunteer effort – they were going on leave in a couple of days' time and were offered the chance of getting off early if they made up numbers on a mining op on the night of 18/19 April.

On that fateful evening the squadron put up nine of its new Lancs as part of a force of 273 to bomb the marshalling yards at Rouen, while six Stirlings were detailed to lay mines in Kiel Bay. Skippering Flt Sgt John McFarland's crew was 26-year-old Flg Off Jim Murray RNZAF, who hauled heavily-laden Stirling III EH955:K off the end of Mepal's runway in the twilight at 20.40hrs and set course for Denmark:

It was quite an uneventful trip out and we laid our veg on time in Kiel Bay and turned for home on a short NW leg which should have taken us to the Danish coast north of Esbjerg.

Without warning the aircraft was raked with cannon fire from beneath – I have a brief recollection of the navigation table being riddled a few feet away. The pilot, Flg Off Jim Murray, and the flight engineer, Sgt Hiram Kahler, were experiencing great difficulty up front controlling the aircraft, and quite soon Jim Murray gave the order to abandon aircraft.

I believe Flt Sgt Douglas Hill, the bomb aimer, was the first out followed by myself and Gordon Irwin, the WOp/AG. As I approached the escape hatch I spoke to Hiram Kahler before I jumped. He was still assisting Jim Murray in an attempt to keep the aircraft flying.

I came to ground quite safely at exactly midnight in a ploughed field on open ground between Toftlund and Gram in southwestern Denmark. My thoughts I remember vividly: my family receiving the dreaded telegram 'we regret to inform you . . . .,' our long awaited leave (never volunteer) and, strangely, my bacon and egg meal which I was going to miss.

I did not see the aircraft crash, but I think the other survivors came down in the vicinity as they were captured almost immediately. Jim Murray, Hiram Kahler and the two air gunners, Sgts P. Woollam and J. Mulligan, did not make it and perished in the crash.

After burying my parachute I walked until dawn and approached a farm house which looked friendly. True enough, I was received with great enthusiasm by the family, especially the 15-year-old son Arne (who was one of our welcome-back party 40 years later).

There appeared to be too much excitement in the district after a couple of days so I was moved to the local schoolhouse where the teacher spoke English and there were plans to have me moved to a more remote agricultural area. But the Danish Underground movement at that particular time had broken down and I was handed over soon afterwards.

I eventually landed in Stalag Luft III at Sagan where I found my surviving two crew members. This was some six weeks after 'The Great Escape' when fifty recaptured PoWs were murdered by the Gestapo, so life was quite subdued for a time.

Gram Churchyard, Denmark: from left to right Arne Carstenson, his mother, John McFarland, the village school teacher and Mrs Elsie McFarland, pictured at the graveside ceremony on 19 April 1984. *J.L. MCFARLAND*

We survived reasonably well on the poor German rations, supplemented by a Red Cross parcel once a month until February 1945, when the camp was suddenly called on parade and we were informed that we were leaving at once as the Red Army was approaching Silesia. We were force-marched in a sorry state to Spremburg and entrained there in wagons for the Bremen area. After a few weeks there the British army was approaching and we left in haste eastwards with our captors. We were eventually released by the advancing British columns and in a few days we were flown back to England.

In 1984 John McFarland and his wife Elsie, together with Mrs Miriam Cohen – sister of Hiram Kahler, the flight engineer – visited Gram churchyard in Denmark where the four crew members who perished in the crash are buried side-by-side. The Danes, who had insisted to the German authorities that the four be interred in the public graveyard, have tended the graves with loving care ever since.

Before her pilgrimage to Denmark, Miriam Cohen was distressed to think that her dear Jewish brother was buried in a churchyard, but when she saw the engraved headstones she realised that the four companions all lay beneath one sky and were at peace – Christianity and Judaism united in death.

As a measure of the high regard in which the wartime dead of the RAF are held by the Danes, the church council erected a special memorial headstone in the Garden of Remembrance to the four dead airmen. It reads: 'They gave their lives so that the people of Denmark should be free.'

Requiem Aeternam Dona Eis Domine: Christians and Jew lie side by side, at peace, beneath one sky. *J.L. MCFARLAND*

A Good
Innings

For an RAF bomber aircraft and its crew to survive more than a handful of operations over hostile territory during the Second World War was good luck, but to become a veteran of over forty ops was to defy fate and, many would have argued, to live on borrowed time.

Although nearly one-third of all Stirlings built were lost through enemy action or accidents, a few soldiered on to become celebrities with air and ground crews alike.

No 149 Squadron's Stirling III EF411 OJ:K forms the backdrop for Plt Off Bob Todd's air and ground crews at Methwold in mid-1944. EF411 joined No XV Squadron in May 1943 before passing to No 149 Squadron the following month, with which she completed at least sixty-nine ops. After service with No 1653 HCU, she was SOC on 24 April.

D. CLARKE

In this cheery photograph taken at Bourn on 11 October 1942, air and ground crews of No XV Squadron pose beside celebrated Stirling I N3669 H-Harry, in recognition of sixty-two ops completed. N3669 was the thirty-fourth aircraft to roll off Shorts' production line at Rochester and was delivered initially to No 7 Squadron on 25 August 1941, before passing successively to Nos 26 CF and XV Squadron, completing a total of sixty-seven ops before its transferral to No 1 Air Armament School as instructional airframe M3637. *A. STOBBS via JR/SBRL*

Pictured here in either May or June 1943 at Downham Market, Stirling I N3721:J of No 218 Squadron is reputed to have flown sixty-one ops – all with 218 – before passing to No 1653 HCU after sustaining damage on the first of the Hamburg fire raids, 24/25 July 1943. It was SOC on 1 May 1944. *J. MCILHINNEY*

Compared to its brothers-in-arms the Lancaster and Halifax, not one Stirling could claim to have flown more than 100 operational sorties during the Second World War. In fact, the highest score – and the scorer itself – is open to some dispute. Of the 2,382 Stirlings built, it is believed that only ten or so achieved more than forty ops each, although the number of aircraft and the operations flown may be more or less.

Another No 149 Squadron Stirling to achieve fame as a survivor was Mk III EE963:N, delivered to No 149 Squadron on 27 August 1943. N-Nuts is reputed to have completed fifty-two ops before transferring to No 1653 HCU. Skipper Hank Woolley and crew painted the legend 'The Nuthouse' on the fuselage door.

From left to right, back row to front: J. Murray, Hank Woolley, Syd Prior, unknown spare gunner, Tom Rollo, Dave Oddy and Ginger Wray. *D. ODDY via JR/SBRL*

Although not reputed to be a high scorer, No 218 Squadron's Stirling III EF133 A-Apple certainly makes an interesting subject on completion of thirty-two ops in late August 1944. Wg Cdr John Overton DFC and his crew are pictured on completion of their tour and have painted their names on the fuselage, together with the number of ops flown to date by A-Apple. *L. TAYLOR via JR/SBRL*

It is indeed very difficult to verify such information without knowing how each individual crew defined a sortie. Even after exhaustive research into available records, it is a fool who makes an emphatic claim on the number of ops flown by a particular aircraft. The benefits of hindsight can be many, but in this instance – and with the piecemeal records available – it puts the researcher at a considerable disadvantage.

The Erk and
the Stirling

L ike the backroom boy in many organisations, the RAF's 'Erk' – any man of the non-commissioned ranks who made up the servicing crews – was very much the unsung hero of the war years. Whether a fitter, labouring in the hangar to overhaul a troublesome engine under the watchful glare of the 'Chiefie'; or a mechanic, freezing to death on a distant dispersal in the sleet and darkness while trying to change an induction manifold by the fading light of a torch, the erk was very much the bedrock on which the foundations of the Service were built.

His pay was poor and his accommodation could vary from a fairly comfortable barrack block on one of the prewar expansion stations to a damp and draughty woodlouse-infested Nissen hut on one of the new stations with dispersed sites. The erk was not born to inherit the glittering prizes and acclaim bestowed upon the glamorous bomber barons or fighter aces, but without him they would quite surely have remained firmly earthbound.

The erk was the uncrowned king of invention and improvisation, an achiever of the impossible, and the Stirling initially caused him much furrowing of the brow, wringing of hands and sucking of teeth. It was quite unlike anything he had experienced before. Indeed, for all who were involved in its construction and operation, the systems of the Stirling were new, relatively untried and prone to some alarming malfunctions. Until the advent of this new giant, the erks of No 3 Group had been working with the small and comparatively simple twin-engined Vickers Wellington, and the Stirling proved a challenge in every sense.

To begin with, it offered four aircooled radial engines against the Wimpy's two, linked to fourteen fuel tanks which fed them with 2,254gals of 100 Octane

Aided by one of the tall stepladders specially built to reach the Stirling's lofty wings, fitters at dispersal attend to a snag on the starboard outer Hercules of a Stirling I during 1942. Each of the Stirling's 52in-diameter Bristol Hercules engines was mounted by a four-point attachment, fixed at the bottom to a huge U-shaped member which extended aft on each side of the nacelle, and at the top by two steel fittings attached direct to the main spar. In the space behind each engine was a selection of pumps, electric motors – including the starter – and a gearbox, all of which required regular servicing by engine, airframe and electrical fitters. But the big question of responsibility always arose when a gearbox went u/s: whose job was it to change it?

IWM CH6311

fuel, compared to the Wimpy's six tanks and 750gals; three power-operated gun turrets had been fitted, bristling with eight 0.303in Browning machine guns for the erk to clean, service and arm, instead of the Wimpy's two turrets and six Brownings; the Stirling was also different in its reliance on electrically-driven motors which in practice proved too lightweight for the heavy-duty tasks they were called upon to perform, like undercarriage retraction; and then there was something called 'Exactor' engine controls. At least the flight mechanics and fitters were familiar with aircooled radial engines and the principles of the Exactor controls. The Wimpy was fitted variously with the Bristol Pegasus and Hercules aircooled radials; the oil cooler shutters on the Wimpy IIIs were operated by the Exactor method.

But if all this was not enough in itself, the Stirling offered armourers a major headache with its huge 42ft 7in bomb-bay divided into three longitudinal cells, together with three bomb cells in each wing inboard of the inner engine nacelles, offering a designed load of 14,000lb compared with the Wimpy's meagre 4,500lb. But not all the problems associated with the Stirling were necessarily big ones. Replacement parts for the Wimpy always fitted – pitot heads, for example – but not so with the Stirling. Screw holes never seemed to line up.

Towering 22ft 9in above the ground on a gangling giraffe-like undercarriage that was prone to collapse without notice, the Stirling was certainly a tall order for the erks who maintained it.

Ray Seeley joined the RAF in March 1942, and after technical training at Squires Gate, Blackpool, he was posted to No 149 Squadron at Lakenheath later that year. As a Flight Mechanic (Engines) he was concerned mainly with Daily Inspections (DIs) to ensure the aircraft in his charge was serviceable for operations at any given time.

Each mechanic was normally allocated a particular engine although, if mechanics were on leave, sometimes more than one engine had to be checked. With the aircooled type of engines fitted to the Stirling, servicing was slightly easier and there were none of the problems with leaking coolant.

The inspections were mainly to look out for any leaks, to check oil levels and clearances, and to ensure the correct operation of controls.

The Bristol Hercules Mk VI: The decision to re-engine the Stirling with the 1,615hp Hercules VI twin-row radial sleeve valve engine was taken in May 1941. This new engine mark featured a revised cooling layout with 12in diameter oil coolers sited below each nacelle, replacing the leading edge tanks.

Extended air intakes positioned above the cowlings contained ice-guards and cleaners. With the Mk VI, wire throttle controls replaced the troublesome Exactors of earlier marks.

The Mk VI engine gave more power at high altitude, but weighed more than the Mk XI. Deliveries of Hercules VI-engined Stirling IIIs commenced in January 1943.
ROLLS-ROYCE

After each inspection a Form 700 had to be signed in which you accepted responsibility for the work you had undertaken on the engine. This form was subsequently checked by the pilot.

The other main task was refuelling, a cold and very dangerous job in the winter if the wings were slippery with frost; it was a long way down to the ground. On the other hand, the high undercarriage was an advantage to us because the propellers were out of normal reach. Another unpleasant job was the replacement of de-icing paste on the leading edges of the wings.

'Kilfrost' de-icing paste was applied to the leading edges of aircraft mainplanes and control surfaces. It took about 15 man hours to coat the mainplane, adding an extra 30lb in weight to the aircraft in the process. It was not particularly effective on mainplanes so its use there was discontinued, but Bomber Command continued applying it on control-surface leading edges only, from June 1944 onwards.

Wally Legard was an electrician on 'B' Flight of No 1651 HCU for over three years from 1942 to 1945. Working out on the dispersals, he was concerned mainly with the DIs and any snags which cropped up with the aircraft in his charge during night flying duties.

Under the watchful eye of Sqn Ldr Ken Major, the station engineering officer, erks salvage what useful parts remain from a bent Hercules engine during 1942. In the background, a Stirling I is prepared for the coming night's operations. IWM CH6528

LAC Ray Seeley (top right) takes a break from his duties to pose for the camera with fellow No 149 Squadron groundcrew at Lakenheath in 1943. The two Royal Navy ratings were typical of many from the 'Senior Service' who were temporarily attached to a number of Stirling squadrons throughout the war to gain experience on radial engines. *R. SEELEY*

At 1651 HCU we were not operational except for a few occasions, and were mostly concerned with training aircrews from OTUs to adjust to the four-engined heavy bombers before posting to frontline squadrons. Our Stirlings mostly did cross-countries and the inevitable circuits and bumps so there were always plenty of electrical snags to keep us busy. Over the years I formed a great attachment to the Stirling. Despite working on the marvellous Lanc after the unit converted to the type in December 1944, I never lost my affection for the great old Stirling.

The Stirling was practically all electrical when it came to the operation of bomb doors, flaps and of course the massive undercarriage, being dubbed by we electricians as 'The Electrician's Nightmare'. The first thing we did on DI was to press the earth indicator lights on entering the aircraft, situated halfway up the fuselage aft of the main spar. If they showed either a positive or negative earth then the search was on to locate it because the aircraft would be deemed unserviceable until the fault was rectified. It was invariably traced to the engines so the wiring of both wings would need to be isolated at the wing roots by the disconnection of all the Breeze circuits until both earth lights came back on. Nine times out of ten the fault would be on the cooling gill motor (one of four) or a starter motor and of course these would need to be replaced.

Mildenhall, 1943: Sgt Bobby Gault holds the starboard outer prop of No XV Squadron's Stirling III BK611 'Te Kooti', during a pause from preparing the aircraft for the coming night's operation.

D. MEPHAM via A. EDGLEY

We had seven or eight aircraft to look after on 'B' Flight so we had plenty of snags to keep us busy. The undercarriage of the Stirling proved to be quite a nuisance at times and it was a common sight at Waterbeach to see an aircraft flying around with one leg up and the other down. On one occasion one of our Stirlings with a faulty undercarriage finally landed after a winding down job by the flight engineer (about 1,000 turns) and it was decided to test the undercarriage. After jacking the aircraft up (which took ages with the medieval gear), the undercarriage would be selected 'UP'; in this particular case the wheels went up perfectly. Trying it several times we could find nothing whatsoever wrong so the aircraft was sent up again for a few circuits. But no. Only one leg would come down. After all this, the aircraft was sent to Marshall's of Cambridge for their attention and we heard no more of it.

On another occasion, a kite that had been doing circuits and bumps was back on the hard pad at dispersal, refuelled and left for the night. There must have been a report on the Form 700 of an oil leak because I noticed the 'Chiefie' (Sgt Nixon, 'A' Flight) walk across and look at the engines to find which one was giving the trouble. He had completed his inspection and cleared the wing when the starboard undercarriage simply collapsed, missing the 'Chiefie' by only inches. I have never seen a man so near to being crushed. He was really shaken.

Another time I was duty electrician on the Chance Light at the end of the take-off runway. This position could be pretty dicey because of the

U/T [under training] pilots on circuits and bumps. On this evening one Stirling was ready for take-off on the runway not far from me when for some reason another Stirling decided to land. In so doing his starboard wheel, which was down for landing, hit the cockpit of the stationary Stirling, taking it completely off and the pilot's head with it.

A happening which remains a mystery to me took place one evening at disperal where a Stirling was being refuelled after flying. A petrol bowser was at one side, and an oil bowser at the other. Suddenly there was a small flash on the wing and the whole lot caught fire. There was, of course, a rapid exodus of bods from the trailing edge of the wing. There was an enormous flash as the petrol bowser went up followed by the oil bowser and the tractor that pulled it. Fortunately, no one was hurt but the aircraft was reduced to a heap of ash. The blame for this was attributed to a refueller's torch when his filament broke and ignited the fuel vapour.

A funny occasion at Waterbeach, when the fear of invasion was in the air, was when someone decided aircraft at dispersal were at some risk and should be guarded. Of course, this fell to the flight groundcrew and was dubbed 'Kite Guard'. After being issued with a rifle, bandolier of ammunition, blankets and a flask of coffee we were transported to our own flight of aircraft at dispersal. One man to each aircraft was the ruling and the Stirling was your home for the night. It doesn't sound so bad but it was very eerie, when every breeze through the nacelles made the strangest of sounds, making sleep quite impossible – not to mention the casualty bed which was as hard as iron. To make matters worse, the following happened and I still feel niggled about it to this day when I bring it to mind.

At around 9pm the orderly officer would come to each aircraft, bang on the door and ask if everything was all right. Each occupant would, of course, be ready at the door to answer – sitting in the pilot's seat he could see him coming from the main camp. On one occasion he came I answered back that everything was okay and he carried on to the next aircraft.

In the morning the WAAF driver would pick us all up and deliver us to the main camp for breakfast, then back to the flight to work. Later in the day in question I was told I was on a charge for not being in the aircraft when the orderly officer came round. To this day I have never understood the reason why. Nevertheless, I was given three days' jankers.

We moved lock, stock and aircraft from Waterbeach to Wratting Common on 20 November 1943, and after Waterbeach, a dispersed camp like Wratting was quite another kettle of fish with mud, and gumboots the order of the day – indeed, every day.

J.F. Hardman was posted to No 214 Squadron at Stradishall in July 1941 as a Flight Mechanic (Engines) and by the summer of 1942 he had undergone further training for promotion to Corporal Fitter 2(E).

From my side of the aircraft the Bristol Hercules engines were superb. Being aircooled with a dry sump (the oil tanks were in the wings), there was virtually nothing to leak, and those leaks we did have were very minor. Bullets and cannon shells only chipped pieces off and we never had an engine unserviceable unless the prop was severely damaged. One engine had a cylinder shot off from the front bank at the top; the piston was still churning up and down in the fresh air. My oppo and I devised a way of changing engines with five men in under four hours – it used to take around eight, so others squadrons came to copy.

Changing the harness for the sparking plugs was a terrible job. In general, most of the other jobs were not at all bad unless you were lying on your back on a trestle out in the snow at night with the East Anglian wind blowing an icy gale as you tried to change an induction manifold by the light of a failing torch.

Engine controls on the earlier marks of Stirling were moved by a kind of hydraulic action known as 'Exactor'. Rubber washers used to give loads of trouble, and to get the throttle on each engine to be level at the same revs was very difficult at times. This applied to mixture and pitch controls as well.

Supervised by a proud 'Chiefie' clad in his workshop coat, air and ground crews of No 218 Squadron put their best feet forward on the mainplane of Stirling III EF133 at Downham Market during 1944. *L. TAYLOR via JR/SBRL*

The last winter of the war in Europe was particular hard. To enable flying operations to continue unabated, it was a case of all hands to the brooms and shovels.

Top: Stirling IVs of No 620 Squadron of Great Dunmow wrapped up against the snow. *NOEL CHAFFEY*

Above: personnel of No 138 (SD) Squadron attempt to dig out a perimeter track at Tempsford, while in the background others can be seen clearing snow from a Stirling. *H. SHAW via K.A. MERRICK*

Above: Through a break in the swirling snow, whipped into a frenzy by the cutting East Anglian wind, stooped figures of No 199 Squadron groundcrew shelter beneath the crouching bulk of a Stirling at North Creake in late December 1944. The extreme conditions in which the groundcrews were expected to work are illustrated graphically in this wintry scene.
C. MUNRO via JR/SBRL

No 214 Squadron groundcrews gather for a group photograph at Stradishall in the summer of 1942, before a newly delivered Stirling I. Cpl J. Hardman is in the middle row, fourth from right.

J. HARDMAN

By comparison with the Rolls-Royce Merlin engine, the Hercules aircooled was the best to work with. Although the Merlin engine was better in overall terms, the Merlin-engined Lancs suffered from all sorts of leaks from their radiators and hoses, and were far more difficult to keep serviceable. Rolls-Royce never got the exhaust stubs sorted out: they burnt out like paper. The studs became more or less welded in the cylinder block and had to be drilled out before oversize studs could be fitted. You could only do the job twice or you were through the head and into the water jacket. Give me the aircooled Hercules any day.

The Stirling itself has been likened to a flying solenoid and was an electrician's nightmare from the start. Early aircraft had a 24V 1,000W generator fitted to each inboard engine, connected in parallel with two 40A hr batteries. Later

aircraft had a 24V 1,500W generator on each inboard engine, connected with four 40A hr batteries. The electrical system was used to operate the main undercarriage and tailwheels, flaps, bomb doors, bomb-release gear, engine starters, cowling gills and propeller feathering motors. With such heavy reliance placed upon lightweight electrically driven motors to operate these systems, these first-generation motors were prone to frequent failure and the batteries to rapid exhaustion.

Hardman continues:

> The Stirling had around 17 miles of wiring plus electric motors by the score. Some of the faults caused by short circuits were unbelievable. Eventually the accumulators had to be disconnected as soon as the aircraft was dispersed, but before this, anything could happen.

We would go out to dispersal and find that one undercarriage leg had collapsed during the time the thing was on its own. Aircraft would try to land with 'one home and one away' with the poor flight engineer trying to wind the jammed leg down, an exhausting task that could take up to 10 minutes to achieve with the gearing used.

One night, going to start engines with a mechanic, we were about 200yds from the aircraft when the rear guns opened up. Fortunately, all guns had to be left pointing skywards so we were all right, but I've never jumped off a bike so quickly in all my life. The electrician had connected up the accumulators ready for a run-up, but the short had taken place after he had left.

On another occasion my aircraft was bombed up with incendiaries fused to detonate at 8ft. Bomb doors were always left open and while we were on the way around the airfield a short caused an SBC full of incendiaries to fall. The distance to the ground was about 12ft so we had a nice fire. The full bomb load plus 2,000gals or so of fuel burned merrily for about an hour, although fortunately there were no HE bombs on board.

When working in the hangar, aircraft had to have jacks under in case a leg started to go up. We had a flight mechanic who was sitting on the dome changing the CSU when the engine turned over and he was thrown to the ground – around 15ft.

On occasions, the electrical problems which plagued the Stirling could prove fatal, as Dr Roland Winfield DFC, AFC, a consultant in Applied Physiology at RAE Farnborough, witnessed at Oakington in 1942. As an RAF doctor he was accustomed to coping with dead and dying aircrew as an inevitable adjunct to operational flying, but sudden and violent death amidst the routine of an ordinary day's work in the hangars made a deep impression on him. The following extract is taken from his book *The Sky Belongs to Them* (William Kimber, 1976).

It was dark. I had been playing squash and my way back to the Mess took me across the tarmac and through one of the hangars. I came out of the dark into the brilliantly lit hangar where one of the Stirlings, A for Apple, was having a defect in its landing gear investigated. The aircraft was supported on trestles and the two front wheels hung limply from the extended oleo-legs, leaving a gap of about 6in between the huge rubber tyres and the concrete floor of the hangar. Three inspection lamps were suspended from the bowels of the Stirling and the light glared outwards, throwing a monstrous shadow of the aircraft upon the white-washed hangar wall. The effect was to produce the likeness of a gigantic insect the shape of a dragonfly or a praying mantis.

Up to his ankles in spring flowers, an armourer of No 620 Squadron at Fairford prepares the four 0.303in Brownings in the Frazer-Nash FN20 rear turret of a squadron Stirling IV, just prior to D-Day. A redesigned and improved version of the FN4 used earlier in the war, the FN20 was popular with gunners and offered armour plating, a movable clear-vision panel and improved ammunition supply. Beneath the turret, attached to the fuselage, can be seen the glider-towing bridle.
N. CHAFFEY

As I crossed the hangar my path brought me alongside the Stirling and, I although I knew I should be late for tea, I couldn't help but stop and look at what was going on. There was a gentle hum of the electrics. The flight sergeant in charge of the maintenance had balanced himself by standing on top of one of the wheels of the undercart and was peering upwards into the housing that contained the undercarriage when it was retracted. I heard him shout to the fitter inside the aircraft 'OK, Bert. Cut the switches. That'll do for now. We'll trace this fault when we've had our tea.'

And those were the last words the flight sergeant ever spoke. It was established afterwards that the fitter had done exactly what he had been told to do and was in no way to blame for what happened. Owing to a fault in the wiring, when the fitter turned the switches off from inside the aircraft the steady hum that I have mentioned suddenly turned into a grinding clatter and the leg of the undercart on which the flight sergeant was perched slowly began to retract itself into the belly of the aircraft, taking him with it. Although it was over in less time than it has taken you to read this paragraph, it seemed a very long time. The folding undercarriage squeezed the life out of the sergeant as effortlessly as it would have crumpled a sheet of newspaper, and as effectively.

A variety of unofficial clothing styles are in evidence in this group of 'A' Flight groundcrew from No 196 Squadron at Shepherd's Grove in March 1945.

J. PARKER

It was all over so quickly that I like to think that the poor man was dead before he was aware of what was happening to him. But the disentangling of his body was a long and messy business and A for Apple was never a lucky aircraft afterwards. She went missing with all her crew on the first operational flight she made after this event.

The height of the Stirling from the ground posed special problems for the bombing up teams. In January 1945, Roy White was an Ordnance Mechanic First Class with the Fleet Air Arm, attached to the RAF at Rivenhall, Essex, home to the Stirling IVs of Nos 295 and 570 Squadrons.

Two-man groups had three Stirlings to look after which meant a good deal of hard work. After loading boxes of belted ammunition to feed the rear turret came the bombing up. The Stirling IV could carry twenty-four 500lb bombs – eighteen in the fuselage bomb-bay and three in each wing cell. The bombs came out from the bomb dump ready fused with a semi-circular lug on the top by which the bombs were hauled up into the bomb-bay. There were seven rows of three bomb racks in the main bay, although only six of these could be used because of centre of gravity problems; and three racks in each wing. The bomb winch had to be

Wyton, 1941: the groundcrew of No XV Squadron's Stirling I N6086:F, 'MacRobert's Reply', gather beneath their charge.

R. ROBERTS via JR/SBRL

Erks at one of Rivenhall's dispersals during 1945 sit for a smoke on a discarded Stirling main wheel tyre.

via B.A. STAIT

Queueing at the NAAFI wagon for a cup of tea and a wad: Rivenhall 1945.

via B.A. STAIT

taken to each bomb station in turn and was very heavy. Because of the narrowness of the Stirling's bomb cells there was only room for one man to operate the winch and secure each bomb at its station. The winch itself was very low geared so consequently it took an age to lift a bomb or container to its position in the fuselage and even longer to the wing cells as they were higher still. Each two-man group therefore had to load a total of seventy-two bombs into three aircraft.

On what were known as 'Night Flight Shifts' we would help to settle the aircrews into their aircraft and watch them take off. We would then go off duty until about one hour before they were due to return. Upon landing and reaching dispersal, the crew would switch off and climb down for a chat with us before debriefing. After they had gone, no one was allowed near the aircraft until the duty corporal armourer and one other armourer had checked the aircraft. This involved making the guns safe before the armourer got down under the aircraft while the corporal hand-opened the bomb-bay doors just wide enough to see inside. With a good torch he peered inside to see if all the bombs had been dropped. It had been known for a bomb to hang up over the target and then release itself with the vibration of the homeward flight or with the bump on touchdown. In that case if would need to be secured.

Every so often we had to come off what was termed 'Operational Duties' and do other work. One such duty was to work in the bomb dump for a period of about two weeks where we had to check every bomb to see if any of the explosive had leaked into the detonator chamber. We had very carefully to insert a finger into the chamber, although too much heat and friction from a finger could have set the bomb off. Similarly, the handling and fitting of the detonator to the bomb was a delicate task because if the detonator overheated it could blow your hand off. It was quite a job to fuse enough bombs for a raid carried out by twelve aircraft and several reserves, with over 300 bombs being loaded.

To Bend
and Mend

'Sebro' was the acronym for the Short Bros Repair Organisation which had its factory at Madingley Road in Cambridge, close to the heart of Stirling country. Although minor repairs to Stirlings were undertaken on their home airfields by either the parent squadron or working parties from the respective builders (Shorts or Austins), major repairs following combat damage or accident were taken on by Sebro if the work involved exceeded the capabilities of the parent squadron. Once repairs had been completed, the various sections of aircraft were taken by road to Bourn airfield a few miles away for reassembly and a test-flight before return to their units.

Headed by a skilled team drafted from Shorts at Rochester, Sebro's small army of workers comprised both men and women, reinforced by airmen with engineering trades, on detachment from the RAF. One of the many youngsters from the Cambridge area called up in 1941 to work the long hours at Bourn mending and reassembling Stirlings was 18-year-old Frances I'Anson:

From 1941 to March 1945 I helped repair and convert Stirlings at Bourn airfield, just outside Cambridge. To learn what was involved, I was sent on a six-month crash course in engineering at Cambridge Technical College, returning to Bourn to put the theory into practice.

Stirlings were brought in to us from the Sebro factory at Madingley Road, and from the surrounding airfields, after they had been shot up on bombing raids. We girls worked with men who were mostly RAF types on release from the Air Force, all sharing whatever jobs needed to be done, from spigot patches where it was a fairly small hole in the bodywork, to perhaps a whole fuselage section which needed a complete

Frances I'Anson worked for Sebro at Bourn from 1941 to 1945, repairing damaged Stirlings. *F. I'ANSON*

Returning from the second 1,000-bomber raid to Essen on 1/2 June 1942, No XV Squadron's Stirling I W7513:R strayed over Antwerp docks at low level, where it was picked up by searchlights and peppered with light flak which seriously wounded the rear gunner and punctured the port main gear tyre. On landing back at Wyton, the punctured tyre caused the aircraft to swerve into soft ground and tip up, with the nose buried in the dirt and tailplane high in the air. The crew had a job getting the injured rear gunner out of the astro hatch, onto the wing, and then down a ladder to the ground. W7513 was repaired and later passed to Nos 149 and 75 Squadrons before it failed to return from a mining op over Kiel Bay on 29 April 1943. *B. ROBERTSON*

A victim of the infamous Stirling Swing, Flt Sgt John Gow RNZAF overcorrected No 149 Squadron's Stirling III BF309 S-Sugar on take-off from Lakenheath on 27 October 1942. The undercarriage collapsed under the heavy side-loadings. *J. BRIGDEN*

rebuild. We could always tell if the gunner had died because we occasionally found fingers and hair in among the blood. After a short time, the men had to do this job at the airfields before the aircraft came into the hangars because it upset us too much.

With my mate called Ted, who was in the RAF, I worked mostly repairing the sheet metal of the bomb-bays – I held the dolly while Ted did the riveting. The most tedious job was replacing the bomb door gearbox. Having smaller hands, the girls would put a little Duralac on their fingers with the nuts on, while their mate on the other side tried to put the bolts through. We could not see a thing, so it was really all done by trial and error.

When the port outer had to be feathered after problems with oil pressure on a raid to Stuttgart on 11 March 1943, Sqn Ldr Ray Glass's 53rd op almost became his last when he eventually made it home in No 214 Squadron's Mk I R9285:J only to overshoot Chedburgh's runway and hit a drainage ditch, tearing off the starboard undercarriage. He managed to bring the aircraft to a stop just in time to avoid hitting a clump of trees, thus avoiding serious injury to the crew and irreparable damage to the airframe.

R9285 was salvaged and sent to Sebro in Cambridge on 19 June where it was repaired and then reallocated to No 1665 HCU. Note the feathered port outer propeller. *R. GLASS via JR/SBRL*

There is some dispute over how No 620 Squadron's Mk IV EF296 met its fate at Fairford on 6 September 1944. Official reports suggest that it burst a tyre on landing and swung off the runway, although other sources point to the aircraft crashing on take-off due to the pitot head cover not being removed. But, whatever the cause, the local children evidently did not miss the opportunity to acquire a souvenir from the wreckage. *N. CHAFFEY*

Like the carcass of some huge beached whale, the sorry-looking remains of No 199 Squadron's Mk III LJ569:C are hoisted aloft before being dismantled by a maintenance unit crew after a take-off crash at North Creake on 15 September 1944, which tore off the starboard wing.

N. PALLANT via JB/SBRL

During early 1944, we began the conversion of Stirlings into paratroop carriers, putting a rail right through the fuselage centre section to the rear escape hatch, on to which could be clipped static lines. We were also involved in fitting the large perspex bubbles beneath the rear fuselage to house the H2S scanners.

I enjoyed working at Bourn, but what I remember most was that nobody quibbled about what particular job they did.

Cloak and
Dagger

From early in 1944 the Stirling began to play a new and increasingly vital role in keeping alive the flame of resistance in Nazi-occupied Europe. From Norway in the snowy north, Denmark, the Low Countries and France, to Italy in the warm south and the mountainous countries of the Balkans and Eastern Europe – even into the very heartland of Nazi Germany itself – Stirlings ranged far and wide under cover of darkness to drop agents and equipment to resistance groups waiting on the ground.

Whereas Bomber Command preferred to operate on moonless nights, the aircraft of the Special Duties (SD) squadrons, supported by the airborne squadrons of No 38 Group, flew at low level during the moon period to assist crews in map reading and the location of remote drop zones (DZs) in tiny forest clearings and corners of isolated fields 'somewhere in Europe'. Even if it came through light or scattered cloud, moonlight was an essential ingredient to lessen the risks of low-flying at night.

For most of the Second World War there were just two dedicated SD squadrons in the UK, equipped for the most part with a variety of cast-off and hand-me-down aircraft types which included the Stirling IV from mid-1944 onwards. These were Nos 138 and 161 Squadrons, based at the cloak-and-dagger airfield of Tempsford near Sandy, Bedfordshire. By the end of the Second World War, No 138 Squadron had undertaken more operations in support of resistance forces than any other RAF squadron.

Dedicated to the SD role of dropping supplies and agents into Occupied Europe, and taking orders from the Special Operations Executive (SOE) headquarters in Baker Street, London, both squadrons were administered by No 3 Group Bomber Command, although No 38 Group (controlled by Fighter

From February 1944 onwards, the airborne squadrons of No 38 Group were engaged in SD operations in support of the two Tempsford squadrons. Flg Off Chas King and his No 196 Squadron crew are pictured standing before their Stirling IV which is bedecked with a large kangaroo emblem and the legend 'It's in the bag.' Below the navigator's window can be seen fifteen dagger emblems denoting supply drops to Resistance forces. *C. KING via K.A. MERRICK*

Command) had a say in the operations undertaken by the two squadrons. Such were the multiple chains of command for the SD squadrons in 1944 that with three different masters with three different – although not dissimilar – objectives, it was no wonder that the crews at squadron level failed to receive enough of the right tools for the job in hand.

During 1943, the Stirling had been selected by the Chiefs of Staff to replace the ageing Halifax IIs and Vs at Tempsford, and of No 148 Squadron in Brindisi, Italy. In October, two prototype Stirling IVs had been delivered to Tempsford for evaluation, although in their present state were deemed by the station and squadron commanders to be wholly unsuitable for SD work. A number of crucial modifications were demanded before the type could be realistically accepted into SD service, including the fitting of a clear perspex nose to enable accurate map reading and supply dropping, modifications to internal fittings in the rear fuselage to allow unimpeded access to the dropping hatch in the aircraft's floor, and increased fuel tankage from the 2,200gal maximum provided in the Mk IV prototypes. Considerable delays ensued and it was not until 11 June 1944 that No 138 Squadron's first modified Stirling IV was delivered, while No 161 Squadron had to wait until early September.

However, by early 1944 the Air Ministry and MAP had been galvanised into action by none other than the Prime Minister himself, Winston Churchill, following petitions from a number of quarters for more SD aircraft, and for larger supplies of weapons and equipment. A prime mover in this matter was a leading SOE agent named Wg Cdr F.F.E. Yeo-Thomas who secured a personal interview with Churchill to put the case for the whole SD cause. To help alleviate this chronic shortage of aircraft during the first half of 1944, Bomber Command made available a number of Stirlings and crews on an ad hoc basis

No 148 Squadron operated in the SD role from Italy in late 1944, alongside No 624 Squadron, as part of No 334 Wing RAF. Four Stirling IVs (LK176, LK181, LK189 and LK249) were ferried out to No 148 Squadron at Brindisi during the autumn of 1944 via Rabat Sale in Morocco, although none was ever used operationally. However, there is some confusion as to whether the plan was simply to re-equip No 148 Squadron with Stirlings or, as some crews were led to believe, a new squadron was to be formed. *J. KLENK*

On 10 March 1945, two Stirlings of No 196 Squadron were involved in a daylight drop of paratroops to a Maquis ski-school in the French Alps, just north of Grenoble. John Hibbs was bomb aimer in one of the aircraft taking part in the exercise, codenamed 'Ibrox':

'Two of our crews were sent to drop members of the Glider Pilot Regiment for ski instruction with a view to a possible future operation in Norway. The other Stirling went in first and we noticed that at the end of his run he was very near the ground. We deduced that the plateau from which the school operated rose at the far end. He hit the ground with his strop guard which was rammed back into the bottom of his aircraft.

'Our troops dropped out on target but the last man hit soft snow. Looking back all I could see was a round hole with his 'chute on top. Fortunately, the Resistance people were on the spot to haul him out quickly.' J. HIBBS

from Nos 75, 90, 149 and 214 Squadrons – recently downgraded from frontline status – to bolster the supply efforts of the hard-pressed Tempsford squadrons. From February 1944, Nos 138 and 161 Squadrons were joined in their efforts by the ten squadrons of No 38 Group which at this point were training for airborne duties in preparation for Operation 'Overlord', of which Nos 190 and 620 Squadrons (Great Dunmow) and Nos 196 and 299 Squadrons (Keevil) were equipped with Stirlings.

However, before Main Force pilots were allowed to drop supplies to the Resistance forces, they were required to fly at least two second dickey trips with an SD crew in order to acquaint themselves with the new techniques and tactics involved. At least one practice drop at Henlow, Bedfordshire, was obligatory to ensure pilots had acquired the skills necessary for dropping containers exactly where they were needed.

In its SD role, the Stirling IV varied little in outward appearance from the standard Mk IV transport variant, both having nose and dorsal turrets removed and faired over. A transparent perspex nose fairing was fitted to improve forward visibility for the navigator and bomb aimer/map reader, and a tubular metal strop guard was attached to the under-fuselage aft of the paradrop hatch to prevent empty parachute bags from fouling the tailplane. An all-up weight of 70,000lb with 2,646gal of fuel was set for the SD version, while the landing weight was restricted to a maximum of 47,510lb. Equipment containers could be carried in the main fuselage and fitted with parachutes and static lines for ejection by the despatcher immediately the agents had jumped.

A number of radio aids were fitted to SD Stirlings to facilitate the crews in their tasks. The Gee box was a standard navigational aid fitted to all bomber and transport aircraft at this point of the war. Another ingenious device, this one called 'Rebecca', had been available from late 1942 for fitting to SD aircraft (and also to motor torpedo boats used in landing agents from the sea). It was effectively a mobile homing device which called up a fixed ground beacon, called 'Eureka', operated by an agent, with a pre-arranged code. A dial in the aircraft carrying the Rebecca set showed how far away and in what direction the Eureka beacon lay. The RAF loved the device for its simplicity, but SOE's agents were less enthusiastic. Eureka's 5ft metal mast surmounting a 7ft-high tripod connected to the radio set would be impossible for its operator to explain away to a German patrol stumbling across it in the corner of a field at night.

At the home of SD operations in the UK, the local residents around Tempsford were, for the most part, blissfully unaware of the highly secret role played by the airfield, its resident crews and motley collection of aircraft. It is perhaps somewhat incongruous that Tempsford should have been chosen for this role, bearing in mind its location between the main LNER railway line and the Great North Road. Security on the airfield was naturally very tight. Unlike the atmosphere at a bomber airfield where crews could exchange views on the

merits, or otherwise, of a particular route to the target as they kitted up in the locker room, there was no free talking or exchange of chit-chat between crews at Tempsford about targets or where so-and-so had bought it. This difference from Main Force operations was further emphasised by a total absence of bombs – just canisters and packing cases filled with a variety of stores which ranged from Sten guns and radios to printing presses and carrier pigeons. And, of course, strange comings and goings in blacked-out motor cars.

As for the crews who flew these SD operations, most had already done one or two tours on bomber squadrons. Geoff Rothwell had joined the RAF in July 1939 on a short service commission and his first posting had been in 1940 to No 99 Squadron at Newmarket, with whom he flew a tour of thirty-seven ops on Wimpys. After an attachment to the RAF delegation in Washington DC in 1942, he carried out a further nine ops with No 75 Squadron and seven with No 218 Squadron during 1943, both on Stirlings, before a spell instructing. As a squadron leader, in June 1944 he joined No 138 Squadron at Tempsford as a flight commander, initially flying Halifaxes, but before long he had converted to Stirlings as they became available.

I found the operational procedure at Tempsford very different from what I had been used to on a normal Bomber Command station. Because of the experience of crews and the individual nature of the job, we were given a certain amount of discretion regarding routes and operating heights, thus adding interest and enjoyment to the task. Pilots, navigators and map readers would discuss details and then clear the route with Intelligence. Our aircraft differed from the normal ones in having the front turret removed and in its place there was a perspex canopy with a seat so that the map reader had an uninterrupted view of the countryside ahead and to the sides. Also, there was the hole in the floor covered by a hatch from which the agents departed over the reception field. I learned later that agents were known as 'Joes' and the hatch in the aircraft was always called the 'Joe hole'.

Special Duties required a high degree of skill from all the crew and there was an awareness of the great responsibility resting on us to deliver the agents and supplies correctly. If we were flying too high when we dropped them they might drift away from the reception on the ground and their safety might be jeopardised. In the case of containers, they would be irretrievably lost if the parachutes became entangled with the trees or they drifted outside the dropping zone. It was an anxious time waiting for the report from the Resistance, and we were always glad when we visited the Intelligence Section and found a message from them to the effect that the drop had been successful. On one occasion I returned from an operation to be told by the Intelligence Officer that they

Opposite, top: Sqn Ldr Geoff Rothwell (third from right), pictured here with his crew on completion of their tour with No 218 Squadron on 26 July 1943, joined No 138 Squadron at Tempsford in May 1944 after a spell instructing at an OTU. He flew sixteen SD ops before crashing in Stirling LK200 on the Dutch island of Texel on 8 September 1944.
G. ROTHWELL via JR/SBRL

Opposite, bottom: No 138 Squadron's Stirling IV LK149:D stands at a wet disperal in early 1945. Little more than 100yds to the right of the aircraft was the barn where agents received their final checks before boarding the waiting aircraft.
H. SHAW via K.A. MERRICK

Seated at a small collapsible map table in the perspex nose of the Stirling was a bomb aimer/map reader whose task, in addition to map reading, was to release the supply containers from the bomb-bays. The success of any SD operation depended largely on his ability to identify pin-points on the ground, keeping the navigator informed of position and degree of drift.

D. BARSBY via K.A. MERRICK

The rear gunner, who could also double as despatcher if need be, assisted in establishing drift by tracking points of reference on the ground down the barrels of his guns.

H. SHAW via K.A. MERRICK

had already had confirmation from the field that the drop had been satisfactory. As often happens when engaged on secret and dangerous work, the morale of the personnel at Tempsford was very high and discipline was maintained through the simple expedient of threatening to post anyone who stepped out of line. It was most effective as I cannot recall taking a single charge during my service with No 138 Squadron.

During June 1944, the squadron was being re-equipped with Stirlings on which I was experienced and so was given the job of checking out the pilots who had flown the type, and converting those who had not. Although the Stirling was vulnerable on normal bombing operations it was ideally suited for SD work at low level as it was very manoeuvrable, particularly in the azimuth plane, and very roomy inside the fuselage.

Tempsford was an unusual station and the briefing procedure was quite different from that in Bomber Command. In the first instance, there was a meeting in a special room in Station Headquarters of the Station Commander, two Squadron COs, four Flight Commanders, two Intelligence Officers and a Met Officer. The room was more like a cupboard than a room as it had no windows and was entered through a door which opened on to a corridor. There was a Yale lock on the door which would be opened to anyone knocking on it who would then be inspected by an Intelligence Officer and, if authorised, the person would be admitted. There was a blackout curtain to be negotiated as the interior was screened from any prying eyes when the door was opened. Even when inside there was little to see as roller blinds covered the walls on which were hung maps of Europe with coloured pins marking the position of every resistance circuit and its codename. The reason for the secrecy and security was now clearly understandable as the whole movement could be in jeopardy if the enemy were to gain possession of the information displayed on the maps. As far as I know there was no leakage about the work done at Tempsford by the SD squadrons or, as they were often called, 'cloak-and-dagger', but when I became a prisoner-of-war I discovered the Germans knew quite a lot about us. As sometimes happens in such circumstances, the enemy probably knew more about what went on than our own side did.

When Grp Capt 'Mouse' Fielden, the Station Commander, arrived, the Met Officer gave us an idea of what weather might be expected over Norway, Denmark, Holland, Belgium and France. From this forecast the CO decided where we would operate and the map of the chosen country was exposed and the Intelligence Officer reported on the circuits which required drops of agents and supplies. The scale of the operation was determined and we returned to our respective squadron offices where the crew lists were compiled and allotted to the various receptions. Flight

Commanders were allowed to operate more or less whenever they wished, providing both were not on the programme on the same night. Squadron Commanders, however, were restricted, and were lucky if they flew more than three or four ops a month.

After briefing, the crew might spend the afternoon checking the aircraft, engines and guns and ironing out any snags before a pre-op meal in the early evening, after which flying kit was drawn and they reported to the Flight

On 10 September 1944, Nos 138 and 161 Squadrons took part in the first of several mass daylight drops of supplies and weapons to Belgian 'Osric' DZs which were manned by the White Army. In this sequence of rare photographs, a member of the Belgian White Army watches a Stirling of No 138 Squadron approach the DZ . . .

... to release its cargo of supplies from the fuselage bomb-bay and through the 'Joe hole' beneath the rear fuselage ...

... while the reception
committee waiting on the
ground quickly gathers the
consignment of cylinders
packed with arms,
ammunition and supplies,
loading them aboard waiting
farm vehicles for concealment
in safe houses and caches
until required for use.
Both 'C' and 'H' type metal
supply containers have been
used in this operation, and
the latter type can be seen in
the foreground. The 'C' type
opened along its axis,
measured just over 1ft in
diameter, 5ft 9in in length,
with four carrying handles,
and when full it could weigh
up to 100kg. Less sturdy, the
'H' type was made up of five
metal drums placed one on
top of the other and secured
by two diametrically opposed
steel rods.

F. BOWMAN via K.A. MERRICK

Offices. The despatcher, however, would be driven to the ramshackle collection of buildings called Gibraltar Farm, at the eastern edge of the airfield, to await the arrival of the agents and it was here that they were prepared for their drop into enemy territory.

Geoff Rothwell continues:

The Joes were in the charge of Army Conducting Officers at a requisitioned country house some ten miles north of Tempsford, in the village of Buckden. The unit, known as Station 61, was administered by the Army and was staffed by FANY (First Aid Nursing Yeomanry) cooks, drivers, etc. When the operation was laid on for particular agents, they were driven in cars, with screened windows so they could not be seen by members of the public, to Gibraltar Farm where they were fitted with parachute harnesses, after they had undergone a thorough examination for any incriminating evidence they might have on their persons which could endanger their safety in the event of a Gestapo check of their credentials. This involved their pockets being turned out to make sure they had no such items as English cigarettes, theatre of cinema ticket stubs, bus tickets, etc. Their clothing was, of course, of authentic Continental design and every precaution was taken to present the agents as genuine citizens of the country to which they were bound. The despatcher would remain with the agents while I returned to the Flight Office to pick up the rest of the crew. Shortly before take-off the agents and despatcher were driven in cars to the entrance door of the aircraft.

The despatcher was a very important member of the crew and had a busy time when we were over the target. He was responsible for shepherding the agents until the time came for them to drop through the Joe hole and if, for any reason, the sortie was aborted and we landed at an airfield other than our own, he stayed with them and protected them from contact with anyone until they were returned to the Army. The despatcher would open the Joe hole hatch when we were approaching the Resistance reception, check the agents' parachutes and attach the static lines so the chute would be pulled automatically out of the pack when they jumped. They would sit with their legs dangling over the hole and when the despatcher's warning light came on he would push them out. He was also responsible for pushing out packages and panniers carried inside the aircraft.

The major Resistance movements were in France so, naturally, most of our operations were to that country. We used two islands in the River Loire near Tours as pin-points and then set course to the next one, and so on, until we finally approached the target area. From now there would be a continual stream of information passed over the intercom as

Supply canisters fall from a Rivenhall-based Stirling in a daylight drop over Norway, late in the war. *via B.A. STAIT*

all crew members, except the despatcher and flight engineer, combined to keep us on course. The crew member who occupied the seat in the perspex nose, with a clear view dead ahead and 90 degrees either side, was a navigator who also acted as the bomb aimer or, in our case since we did not carry bombs, the one who also released the containers. He had received special training in the art of map reading and had a small collapsible table on which to rest his maps which could be illuminated by a dull, red light on a flexible arm for easy manipulation. Once over enemy-occupied territory the success of the operation depended to a large extent on the ability of the map reader to identify pin-points on the ground and keep the navigator informed of our position and degree of drift. The rear gunner was also able to assist through tracking points of reference down the barrels of his guns. As we neared the reception we would look for a prominent landmark decided upon earlier, such as a distinctive woodland or crossroads, and commence a timed run from there to the reception.

From the last pin-point the map reader was in sole charge and guided me in much the same way as a bomb aimer did on a bombing run until I was able to see the lights of the field ahead. The reception party laid out three dim lights with a fourth forming a letter L, from where the signaller would operate. As soon as I saw the lights ahead of us I flashed the code letter on the aircraft's identification lamp and trusted I received the correct reply to the challenge. This procedure was necessary as the Germans had infiltrated some circuits and might lie in wait to capture agents and supplies as soon as they were dropped. This happened on a large scale in the Dutch Resistance and many agents were lost.

On receipt of the correct signal I opened the bomb doors, warned the despatcher we were running up on the reception area, lined up with the lights which should be into wind, and approached at 300–500ft. At the appropriate time the map reader/bomb aimer pressed the bomb release and the containers dropped from the bomb-bays, parachutes opened, and on an ideal operation, landed beside the lights for collection by the reception committee. Sometimes, if the crew were unskilled or conditions unfavourable, the containers were known to drift outside the reception area causing members of the ground party considerable problems, particularly if the parachute was caught up in trees. The despatcher pushed out the Joes if we were carrying any, the panniers if we were not, attempting to get out as many as possible to reduce the number of runs needed to complete the drop. As soon as the final run had been made we flew away from the area as our presence was a danger to the Resistance workers. If we spent too long over the field the German radar might get a fix on the locality so we used to circle some distance away hoping to put the enemy off the scent.

One night the reception which was our objective was under attack when we arrived on the scene. We circled to see whether we could provide any assistance but, unfortunately, we could not distinguish friend from foe, and I had to tell my rear gunner to hold his fire. It was difficult to tell exactly what was happening as there were lights on the roads and gun flashes – not directed at us, we hoped! I considered firing at the vehicle lights but remembered that the Resistance were often able to use transport to carry away the containers so, in the end, we decided against any interference and abandoned the sortie. Some time later we received a message to the effect that the Gestapo had been tipped off that a drop was due to take place and were on their way to the field when we appeared. Luck was on the side of the Resistance members as all escaped, but the field had been compromised and could not be used again.

The return journey was a repeat of the outward one, flying from one pin-point to another and trying to keep away from trouble by following the track we had worked out. We felt relatively safe at the height we flew, providing we knew where we were, but if we strayed off course there was a danger of passing over defended areas and attracting light flak. We

With flaps fully out and props at fine pitch, a Stirling IV of No 138 Squadron is brought in for a wheeled landing at Tempsford in late 1944. Wheeled landings (tail up) were recommended for the Stirling – compared with three-pointers for the Lanc and Halifax – because of the tendency of the tall undercarriage to collapse under side-loadings.

J. BREEZE via JR/SBRL

reckoned nightfighter attacks were unlikely because of our being a single aircraft and the difficulty of interception and combat at low level. They preferred their targets to be mainstream bombers at around 20,000ft when they could be vectored by radar and their prey illuminated by searchlights. This was the reason we were always happiest when there was a bomber force operating when we were.

However, we were not totally immune from fighter attacks and my wireless operator had an amazing experience when flying with another crew on a Danish operation. They were lined up for a run when a Junkers Ju88 came up behind them and opened fire, hitting wings and engines with tracer and cannon. The quick-thinking pilot went straight ahead and crash-landed on the reception field. I think all managed to escape from the aircraft and, in between strafings by the Ju88, the Resistance spirited them away and passed them down the escape route to Sweden. My wireless op was back at Tempsford about three weeks later. So, although this is the only case to my knowledge, a nightfighter attack could not be entirely ruled out and such an occurrence could have been responsible for some casualties because we were seldom able to establish the cause of an aircraft failing to return.

While stationed at Tempsford, No 138 Squadron dropped 995 agents into occupied Europe. One such agent was Jack Grinham, a sergeant driver/radio operator with the Royal Armoured Corps, who was detached to SOE in 1944. He belonged to one of the top-secret three-strong 'Jedburgh' units which comprised a British or American officer, a French officer, and an NCO radio operator who could be of any of these nationalities. Trained in demolition and guerrilla tactics, ninety-three Jedburgh teams were parachuted into enemy-occupied France between D-Day and the end of September 1944 to assist Resistance groups. They called in supply drops, and advised on the most efficacious tactics to complement the battle plans of the regular Allied ground forces. Jedburgh teams used forenames as codenames, such as 'Cecil', 'Maurice' or 'Stanley'; Jack Grinham's team was codenamed 'Stanley' and dropped from a Stirling IV of No 138 Squadron over eastern France on the night of 31 August 1944.

Sgt Jack Grinham was one of a three-man 'Jedburgh' unit, codenamed 'Stanley', dropped into France by a Stirling of No 138 Squadron on the night of 30/31 August 1944. *J. GRINHAM*

Briefing was a rather hurried one and we left London in great haste mid-afternoon after being told our op was on; our DZ was just north of the village of Rivières les Fosses, 15 miles south-southwest of Langres in the Haute Marne region of eastern France.

Teams were briefed individually and only one team of Joes went per aircraft. None of us knew where any other team was going or when. The radio operators were mostly NCOs of sergeant rank; I was one of those belonging to team 'Stanley'.

We'd grabbed our kit including radio (all personal to us) and were briefed in the truck as we drove north to Tempsford, not to the airfield but to a closely-guarded house nearby where the briefing was completed and I received my personal radio briefing.

All the kit had been taken to the airfield for packing. Although we dropped in uniform we were kitted out with civilian clothes – all genuine Continental stuff – as well as forged identity cards and other documents. We were thoroughly searched for anything that might give us away if captured. The only British document I carried was my Army Book (AB64), no bus tickets, cigarettes or anything that would indicate I'd come from England. Once in France we all wore civvies until it was safe

Although very few 'Jedburgh' teams took civilian clothing with them into France or carried false documents, Jack Grinham assumed the identity of one Octave Grimaldi, a manual labourer. *J. GRINHAM*

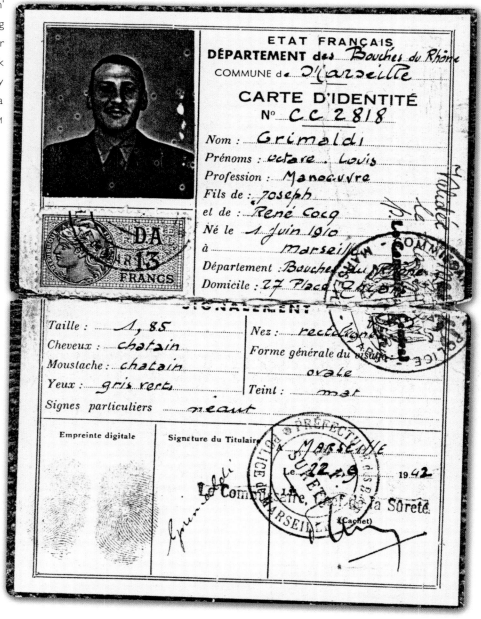

to wear uniform; this made us less conspicuous until it was safe to do so and less of a danger to those who received us. We had a slap-up meal at this house and then went to the airfield.

Once there we were treated with quiet efficiency, great friendliness, and kitted out with parachutes, spine pads and para helmets which we had to put on before boarding the Stirling which was to take us to France. The crew were business-like although very friendly. Once in the air the only one I saw was the despatcher.

It was dusk as we crossed the English coast; searchlights picked us up and it scared me. Thoughts of being fired upon by our own ack-ack did not appeal. It was surprising how much light was thrown up, but the despatcher soon reassured us all was well, with no danger. After that he told us to get our heads down and sleep. There were huge quilts to roll ourselves in, but sleep – I was much too excited for that!

I can't remember just how long the trip took, maybe three or four hours, but it was a very smooth one despite being noisy and cold. Not long before our ETA over the DZ we were provided with a lovely hot coffee from huge flasks; a super thought.

On approach to the DZ our static lines were hooked up, everything checked and rechecked. The huge doors in the floor were opened, almost big enough to chuck a billiard table through, and we could see the reception committee's lights on the ground below in the bright moonlight.

We were given the usual 'Running in – Action Stations', and on our final run the green light came on and 'Go!' Out we went into the night. Capt Craster (later Maj) was No 1, I was No 2, with Lt Carlière (later Col) No 3. (Carlière was his *nom de guerre*; his real name was Cantais, something I didn't know until 40 years later.) We were bang on time and target. There were two French *sous-officiers* [approximately 2nd lieutenant equivalent] who jumped with us as Nos 4 and 5 although they were not in our team. They had their own briefing and left us later that day.

I clearly remember the Stirling on its next circuit dropping its huge load of containers and packages; it looked as though the aircraft was falling to pieces. Within the next few weeks we had two further drops of arms and supplies, both bang on time and target. I only wish I knew who the crew were so I could thank them for their good service. We Joes owe a lot to them.

After the Jedburgh campaign in France came to an end in September 1944, Jack Grinham returned to England and was promptly posted straight out to the Far East where he joined Force 136 based in India for SD operations in South East Asia. He survived to enjoy the fruits of the peace he had fought so hard to win.

But while Jack Grinham had kept the return portion of his ticket into occupied Europe and used it to good effect, unbeknown to Geoff Rothwell the last flight he was to make of his tour with No 138 Squadron would be a strictly one-way affair.

In early September, Geoff completed his seventieth op and was earmarked for promotion to wing commander and the command of the squadron with the imminent departure of Wg Cdr Wilf Burnett to a staff appointment. Before becoming chained to a desk, Geoff wanted to get in one last op, which he duly cleared with Wilf Burnett before attending the briefing on 8 September. Flying in Stirling IV LK200, Geoff and his crew were to fly two Joes codenamed 'Draughts' and 'Backgammon' with a load of carrier pigeons to a DZ in the Alkmaar district of Holland. It appeared a straight-in-and-out job and Geoff felt a little embarrassed to be finishing with an easy op, such as would usually be given to a freshman crew.

Our take-off time was quite late, around 10.30pm, and when we were halfway across the North Sea I saw ahead of us a gigantic cumulo-nimbus cloud, far too extensive to fly around, so I decided to try to climb above it. I soon realised the task was far beyond the capability of a heavily-laden Stirling and so I flew straight ahead into the cloud. It was extremely rough and we were going up and down like a yo-yo and being so tossed about by the turbulence I began to fear structural damage to the aircraft. Eventually, I decided as a last option to go down to sea level and try to get underneath the cloud. We broke out of the cloud base at about 300ft but found ourselves in driving rain, making it impossible to see anything ahead or below. I turned on my landing light and through the sheeting rain I saw what poets call 'the tempestuous sea' beneath us. I flew for some time and then, suddenly, we were in bright moonlight and clear skies.

When operating over the Netherlands we used to pinpoint our position by a horseshoe-shaped bay on the undefended island of Vlieland, one of the Friesian group bordering the Zuider Zee. From Vlieland we set course for the end of the causeway which stretches across the vast expanse of water, forming an inland sea and joining the peninsula of North Holland with Friesland on the east side. From our accurate pinpoint over Den Oever we flew direct to the reception and had no difficulty in completing the drop, after which we threw out our pigeons in their little cardboard cylinders over populated areas, returned to our pinpoint on the causeway and altered course to bring us over Vlieland. I congratulated myself on the ease of the operation and looked forward to my 'operational egg' back at Tempsford. As in all things, it is wise not to start counting the poultry too soon!

We were flying at a height of about 300ft when the map reader came on the intercom to tell the navigator he could see the bay on Vlieland ahead and that we were a little port of track. Roddy McKitrick (Mac) the navigator was a meticulous person who liked to see things for himself and, on this occasion, he came forward from his chart table and stood beside me to look through the windscreen. Suddenly, without any warning, a number of incidents occurred which have become indelibly etched in my memory as I have relived them so often.

The Stirling seemed to stop as though it had hit some very solid object. From the instruments I saw the airspeed indicator show we had picked up speed and I instinctively hauled back on the control column but felt an approaching stall. I then realised the instrument was inoperative and the needle had simply dropped to the bottom of the scale, showing something like 250kts and making me think we were in a dive. I levelled off and attempted to fly the aircraft but had to contend with severe damage. The starboard inner propeller had flown off and fire had broken out in the engine; fuel pressure was lost on all engines except the port inner; the aileron controls were almost ineffective; and it was very difficult keeping the wings level.

We were losing height rapidly and I was unable to keep on a straight course. I remember asking Mac for an emergency course to base but realised there was no hope whatsoever of avoiding a crash-landing. We were still over water and too low to bale out so I told the crew to stand by for a ditching. As we got lower I saw from the light of the fire, which had spread into the wing, that we were flying over sand dunes and dead ahead was a hillock into which we were obviously going to crash. I pulled hard back on the control column and heard Mac say 'The starboard wing is stalling.' I remember no more of what occurred but it would appear we avoided hitting the dune head-on due to the wing touching the ground and slewing the aircraft round to starboard.

After crashing at a speed of 100–150kts it would be surprising if I were able to recount clearly what happened and it is from a hazy recollection that I try to recapitulate the events. When I gained consciousness I found myself suffocating with my head buried in the sand. I had sand in my eyes and ears, up my nose, in my mouth, and a severe pain in my side. I pulled myself out of the dune and found I had no flying helmet and only one shoe. When I had cleared my eyes I saw that I was standing in the middle of wreckage strewn all around with the starboard wing blazing furiously, having broken off the fuselage. I can remember being astonished to find I was alive and set out to try to find the rest of the crew.

The first person I came across was Mac, lying on his back groaning but relatively unhurt, apart from a rather nasty hole in his chin and what looked like a broken thumb. I found Derek Shaw, the flight engineer, lying stretched out on top of a sand dune, unconscious and breathing very heavily, with what I took to be a severe head wound. I decided not to move him in view of his critical condition and went in search of the rest of the crew.

I was afraid the petrol tanks would explode as the fire was very fierce and I told Mac we must get away as quickly as possible. I could find no trace of the fuselage, which appeared to have disintegrated. However, I came across Sgt Wilmott, the despatcher, in a sitting position but with one leg sticking out at a most unusual angle and it was obvious that it was broken. He said he felt all right except for his leg which he could not move. I told him it would be wise not to try to move him and I expected the Germans would soon be on the scene as the fire could be seen for miles around. I felt uncomfortable at leaving him alone but nothing could be achieved by remaining. He seemed quite content and said he would be all right so I went back to where I had left Mac.

We were both feeling the shock of the crash but pulled outselves together and started walking across a field. We had raging thirsts, probably due to having our mouths full of sand. We had no plan as we did not know whether Vlieland was inhabited by the Dutch, but an idea was forming in the back of my mind that if we could obtain a boat of some sort we might manage to get down the coast as we believed the British Army was on the Belgian/Dutch border somewhere south of us. A fanciful idea but the best I could produce under the circumstances.

Geoff and Mac attempted to seek sanctuary from a frightened couple at an isolated house and were surprised to learn that they were at a place called De Cocksdorp on the island of Texel, and not Vlieland as they had assumed. Having no wish to endanger the couple, they kept walking until dawn when they came to a farmyard where they met a man who spoke English. He told them it would be impossible to avoid capture since the Germans had found the crashed Stirling the night before and realised some of the crew were missing. In any case, all the boats on the island were in German hands and nobody could help them. Realising there was nothing to be done, the pair turned themselves in to the Germans.

Unfortunately, Geoff Rothwell's wireless op, map reader and rear gunner were killed in the crash, but his engineer, navigator and despatcher survived with him to enjoy the enforced hospitality of the Third Reich at Stalag Luft I.

What it was that caused their Stirling to crash remains a mystery to this day.

One other squadron was operating Stirlings in the Special Duties role in England during 1944–5 and that was No 199 Squadron at North Creake, Norfolk. It had no involvement with the clandestine activities of the two Tempsford squadrons, although its work was of an equally sensitive nature.

The role of No 199 Squadron was to jam German radar transmissions with the powerful Mandrel electronic jamming equipment fitted to its Stirling IIIs. The squadron had been transferred to No 100 (SD) Group from No 1 Group on 1 May 1944 to augment the activities of No 192 (SD) Squadron based at

North Creake, 1944: Two Stirlings sit at No 199 Squadron's 'A' Flight dispersal, waiting for the call to arms that will surely come. In the foreground is Mk III LJ543:J with fifty-eight ops to its credit. In the background is LJ542:G, known as 'The Gremlin Teaser', with a tally of sixty ops. Both aircraft are fitted with 'Mandrel' and 'Shiver' radio counter-measures (RCM) equipment. *199 REGISTER via SAA*

In this photograph of No 199 Squadron's Mk III LJ565 taken at North Creake in June 1944, a good view can be had of the various RCM attachments to the squadron's Stirlings.

Immediately aft and below the rear access door is the IFF aerial, while the two aerials beneath the fuselage to the left of the picture are part of the 'Mandrel III' array. This device was designed to spot-jam enemy early-warning radar in the 148–196MHz band. Beneath the roundel can be seen the 'Window' chutes.

Lounging in the grass beside Q-Queenie are, from left to right: Ben Riggs; Al Wood, navigator; Will Hancock, pilot; Olly Pask, flight engineer; Phyllis Noble and Pamela Moran.

Q-Queenie flew thirty-nine ops with No 199 Squadron and was one of several Stirlings transferred briefly to No 171 Squadron in September 1944 until its Halifax IIIs arrived. *W. PACHOLKA via JR/SBRL*

No 199 Squadron's Stirling III LJ514 B-Beer, is pictured on a RCM sortie during 1944. More than seventy ops were flown by this aircraft. It was SOC on 2 May 1945.

nearby Foulsham. Its aircraft were specially fitted with three different types of jamming and navigational equipment: Mandrel, which generated electronic 'noise' to jam German early-warning radar systems; Shiver, a device designed to jam the enemy's Ground Controlled Interception and Gun Laying radars; and Gee. This equipment was fitted to the squadron's Stirlings by the experts in electronic warfare at Defford (TRE) and Foulsham (BSDU).

However, not all of the squadron's sorties were ones employing Mandrel. With the creation of the Special Window Force in July 1944, No 199 Squadron became involved in 'windowing' operations with available aircraft from No 100 Group's other heavy squadrons (192 and 214). The aim of the force was to create a fake bomber stream by dropping Window to a preset pattern, thereby deceiving enemy radar operators.

No 199 Squadron was raised to a three-flight status in August 1944 but, due to delays in equipping the newly-formed No 171 (SD) Squadron with Halifax IIIs, one flight of Stirlings was temporarily transferred to the squadron to act as a nucleus. Stirling sorties with the new squadron continued until 21 October, by which time it had received its full establishment of Halifaxes.

In March 1945, No 199 Squadron began to convert to the Halifax III, flying its final Stirling sortie on 14 March – the last Stirling operation to be flown by Bomber Command.

Opposite, top: These were the special signal technicians on Nos 171 and 199 Squadrons who maintained the top secret RCM equipment fitted to the aircraft.

Pictured at North Creake in June 1944 are, *back row:* LAC Dick Masters, AC Bosworth, LAC Aldworth, LAC Ivor Birch, LAC Mike Connolly, AC 'Dickey' Bird, LAC Dunthorn, LAC Breed.

Centre: LAC George Reed, Cpl E. Nicholas, Cpl Joe Rose, Sgt M. Major, Cpl Len Boxell, LACW Yvonne ?, Cpl Light.

Front: Cpl Mason, Cpl Wyatt, LAC Cosgrove, LAC Pete Ballard, LAC Terry Buckley, LAC Freddie White, LAC Tutt. *E. NICHOLAS via JR/SBRL*

Opposite, bottom: RCM Crew: Phil Bowering's No 199 Squadron crew completed over forty ops except for 'Baldy' Baldwin, the bomb aimer. He broke his arm on a pub crawl, had it set wrongly by an Army medical officer and was invalided back to Canada. From left to right: J. Stokie RAAF, rear gunner; Joe Gibbons, wireless operator; Claud Allen, flight engineer; 'Curly' Brown, mid-upper gunner; Norman Pettit RCAF, navigator; Phil Bowering RAAF, pilot; D. 'Baldy' Baldwin, bomb aimer. *W. BROWN via JR/SBRL*

"MACROBERT'S REPLY"

Perhaps one of the best-known Stirlings of the early war years, N6086 was allocated to No XV Squadron on 15 September 1941 and formally handed over to one of the squadron's pilots, Flg Off Peter Boggis (left), in a ceremony at Wyton on 10 October. The aircraft bears the coat of arms of the MacRobert family and the legend 'MacRobert's Reply.'

But the story behind the picture is a tragic one. To perpetuate the memory of her three sons – one who died in a flying accident in 1938, the other two on operations with the RAF during the war – Lady Rachel MacRobert of Douneside and Cromar, made funds available for the purchase of three Hawker Hurricanes and one Short Stirling, N6086. (The three 'MacRobert Fighters' were Hurricane Mk IIcs and served with No 94 Squadron in the Western Desert in 1942.)

Like many of its contemporaries, 'MacRobert's Reply' came to a sorry end. Swinging on take-off from Peterhead in early February 1942 and ploughing into the heavily banked-up snow bordering the runway, it crashed into a parked Spitfire before losing its port wing and undercarriage.

N6086 was taken south to the Sebro works at Cambridge for extensive repairs, from where it re-emerged to see service with No 1651 HCU before finally crashing at Oakington on the night of 14 March 1943 after suffering an in-flight engine failure.

A replacement aircraft to carry the 'MacRobert's Reply' legend and coat of arms was allocated, but like the brave young men it sought to commemorate W7531, too, went missing. Flak brought it down on a mine-laying op in the Baltic on 17 May that same year. *IWM CH3947*

No 620 Squadron's 'Cheers for Beer at the Getsuminn' is given the thumbs-up seal of approval from its pilot, Tom Herbert.

This well-endowed and curvaceous birdwoman named 'The Gremlin Teaser' adorns the nose of No 199 Squadron's LJ542, G-George, the handiwork of the aircraft's flight engineer, Flt Sgt Ted Allen, during 1944.

W. BROWN via JR/SBRL

'Yorkshire Rose II' was LJ566, a Mk IV of No 620 Squadron, the regular mount of Plt Off Derek de Rome RAAF, during 1944–5. After allocation to the squadron at Fairford on 18 May 1944, it flew a total of more than thirty ops – all with No 620 Squadron – but suffered battle damage on a resupply drop to Arnhem on 20 September. Returning to the squadron two weeks later, it saw out the rest of the war without further mishap.

The operational tally beneath the cockpit records twenty-nine SOE drops, two glider-towing sorties (D-Day and Arnhem), and two bombing ops. *N. CHAFFEY*

'The Bushwacker' was an Australian-crewed Stirling IV LJ995:H of No 295 Squadron, pictured at Rivenhall in the winter of 1944–5. The emblem on the nose depicts an old Aborigine wearing a tall hat, sitting on a rock clutching a bottle of liquor, while cooking a lizard on a stick over a camp fire. The aircraft has flown a variety of operations, with twelve SOE drops denoted by dagger emblems, three SAS drops signified by winged daggers, and a single glider-tow emblem for participation in the Arnhem drop.

'The Bushwacker' did not survive to see the end of the war: it swung on take-off at Rivenhall on 4 February and hit some trees before it crashed and exploded. *F. PRIEST via K.A. MERRICK*

No 295 Squadron's 'Goofy II', EF446, was built originally as a Mk III, but became one of many converted to Mk IV standard. Delivered initially to No 90 Squadron on 27 June 1943, EF446 passed briefly to No 570 Squadron before joining No 295 Squadron on 3 August 1944 to complete a total of thirty-one ops. *J. SWALE via JR/SBRL*

A Change
of Role

When it became apparent that the Stirling lacked any potential for development as a bomber, the Air Ministry began to look at its suitability as a possible glider tug and paratroop transport to replace the Albemarle and Whitley types currently fulfilling these roles.

In April 1943, trials were undertaken with Stirling I BK645 to assess the type's ability to tow a loaded Horsa glider. Performance figures were very promising – even at this early stage and without the removal of turrets – and the Stirling suffered none of the engine overheating problems associated with the twin-engined Albemarle. Further tests followed with the first two Stirling Mk IV conversions (EF503 and EF506) which served as prototypes.

Shorts prepared three schemes for Stirling transports, the preferred Plan 'A' calling for the initial conversion of large numbers of existing Mk IIIs into Mk IVs on the factory production line or at RAF maintenance units, to be used as tugs or troop transports. The changeover to completing Stirlings as Mk IVs – Plan 'B' – began at Belfast in December 1943, with EF317 becoming the first of 577 Mk IVs to be built (including Mk IIIs converted to Mk IVs).

The new Mk IV differed from previous builds in a number of ways, the most obvious of which was the removal of the nose and dorsal gun turrets and the replacement of the nose turret with a transparent perspex fairing. A 6ft x 4ft hatch in the floor of the fuselage just forward of the existing crew entrance door allowed easier and safer egress for paratroops than was hitherto the case with types like the Whitley or Dakota. A retractable tubular metal-framed strop guard was mounted beneath the fuselage aft of the hatch to prevent empty parachute bags and metal parachute strops from bashing against the fuselage or tailplane in the slipstream and causing damage. Once all paratroops had

Displaying the basic modifications of deleted gun turrets common to the Mk IV, LJ512 was used by the Controller for Research & Development, No 304 Ferry Training Unit and finally No 525 Squadron at Lyneham for intensive trials in airline operations between May and July 1944. However, LJ512 differed from the standard Mk IV in several ways: the tail turret was removed and replaced by a transparent perspex fairing, while no strop guard or glider-towing bridle was fitted either.

IWM MH5152

jumped, these could be winched back on board by the despatcher, and the guard retracted manually by use of a raising/lowering arm in the fuselage floor.

For glider towing, a horseshoe-shaped metal towing bridle was fitted aft and below the horizontal stabilisers, with three points for connecting tow ropes and a provision to link into the tug's intercom by means of an audio lead and plug. An intercom wire was woven into the tow rope, connecting the glider and tug, but in practice this wire often broke through the stresses placed upon it in training exercises by the acts of towing, frequent casting off and subsequent recovery of the rope for re-use.

John Hill was an engine fitter with Nos 6 and 8 Maintenance Units (MUs) at Woburn Park from early 1944. In the months leading up to D-Day he was involved in the feverish activity to convert factory-fresh Stirlings to the Mk IV glider-tug configuration.

Woburn Park in Bedfordshire, country seat of the Dukes of Bedford, had been requisitioned by the MAP as a Satellite Landing Ground (SLG) early in the war and became one of fifty such sites spread across Britain for storage and preparation of replacement aircraft for the RAF. The sites were carefully concealed from prying Luftwaffe reconnaissance aircraft by the painting of dummy hedges across the grass landing strips and construction of hangars to resemble village houses or barns. Designated No 34 SLG, Woburn Park was used by Nos 6 and 8 MUs for the storage and conversion of Stirlings, and towards the war's end was scheduled to receive some 174 Stirlings. The breaking up and scrapping of these aircraft began with the return to peace and continued until May 1947 when the RAF finally left Woburn Park.

One day in February 1944 I found myself bound for an unknown destination along with twenty or so other bods, travelling down from Scotland and eventually landing up at Bletchley in utter darkness and not having a clue as to where we were. The RTO and Chiefie organised some lorries and after a short trip we were deposited in the middle of a big park. After scouting around we came to a lodge and found out that we were in Woburn Park.

Dramatically silhouetted against the dusky cloudscape of a winter's afternoon in late 1943, an unidentified Stirling III prepares to land. Fitted with a glider-towing bridle, it is probably one of several Mk IIIs converted for glider-towing trials to determine the Stirling's suitability for the role. *IWM CH11683*

In the centre of the park was a vast open space some ¾-mile long and ¼-mile wide surrounded by all species of trees, used as a landing strip before the war by the Duchess of Bedford. There was a small wooden hangar and a wind sock on a tall pole at the edge of the landing strip, and at the top end of the park was Woburn Abbey, inhabited by dozens of WRENS who were kept under close supervision because of their work at the Communications HQ at Bletchley Park.

We'd only been there a couple of days, organised our tool kits and marked out a landing strip, before the first Stirlings started lobbing in three or four at a time, all brand new from the factory. We always knew when they were coming because the old Anson that ferried the ATA pilots about used to touch down first. Our first surprise came when we saw some of the pilots – a couple of very slight and girlish ladies. We hadn't thought that such big jobs could be handled by women. How wrong we were.

As engine fitters we were very soon working around the clock, from dawn to dusk, ironing out oil and fluid leaks, and rough running. Twelve and 14hr days were the norm. However, the main work to be carried out was the fitting of 'gates' that could be lowered beneath the fuselage aft of the paras' exit hatch in the floor. The gate was a contraption made of tubular steel dropped down and held in place by a strut and pin, designed to trap the trailing static lines from the parachutes and stop them whipping up into the tailplane and causing damage.

When aircraft were ready for air testing, the park ranger – mounted on his lovely little cob, with slouched hat and rifle, like a real cowboy – would gallop up and down the airstrip chasing off any small herds of deer that had grazed into the danger area.

The fire tender was also pressed into service but, notwithstanding the precautions, the inevitable happened one day when a Stirling made an unheralded landing and managed to make venison of five or six Chinese Water Deer. It was the first time we'd tasted venison and it helped our rations out very nicely!

After a few months – and if we could keep ahead of our work – we were given time off and became very friendly with the WRENS who invited us to a dance in Woburn. We were a right scruffy lot, living as we were with no 'Best Blue' handy. They had really worked hard and provided a lovely buffet. A trio of elderly ladies from the village provided the music and the 'dance hall' was one of the large cloisters in the Abbey where all the paintings and statues were draped in purple material. It was an eerie setting for a 'hop'. Very little dancing was done but a few short romances developed.

We had an idea that D-Day was not far off when we were informed that all Stirlings had to be ready and serviced at two hours' notice. After

a couple of false alarms they were all spirited away by RAF types. All except one solitary jinxed kite. Everything that could go wrong with it went wrong. It finished up being a provider of spare parts and for all I know it's still in Woburn Park!

No 299 Squadron at Stoney Cross was the first squadron to receive the new Mk IV in January 1944, followed closely by Nos 190, 196 and 620 Squadrons – the latter two having left Bomber Command in November 1943 to reinforce the new No 38 Wing, shortly to become No 38 Group.

During the following month the four squadrons reached full strength, operations commencing on 3/4 February when No 196 Squadron despatched two Stirlings on a night supply drop to French Resistance groups. Over the next few months and until the end of the war, the Stirling squadrons of No 38 Group would be involved in a variety of Special Duty operations to dropping zones in France, the Low Countries and Scandinavia.

Large-scale training exercises with Horsa gliders and crews from the Army's Glider Pilot Regiment began in February in preparation for the imminent Allied invasion of north-west Europe, now little more than a few months away.

Constructed initially as a Mk III, EF309 was one of a number converted to Mk IV standard before delivery to No 196 Squadron on 25 April 1944. It flew eleven operations with the unit and suffered substantial damage after belly-landing at Keevil on 19 July 1944, but continued in service after repair, only to be SOC on 5 July 1947.
J. GRAF via JR/SBRL

Stirling and Horsa crews trained hard for the day when they would pit their skills against an equally determined and resourceful enemy. However, there were some lighter moments to the training routine as Bill Higgs, a staff sergeant in 'D' Squadron of the Glider Pilot Regiment, recalls.

During training behind Stirlings prior to operations, there was a bit of a competition between the glider pilots of different squadrons as to who could go highest in a glider. Information reached us in 'D' Squadron at Keevil that heights of 9, 10 and 11,000ft had been reached.

My squadron commander, Capt Ogilvie, informed me that Stirling K-King had just had an engine overhaul and was in tip-top condition. The next order I received from him was to go up behind K-King in a Horsa and beat the other squadrons' records.

The skipper of the Stirling, Flg Off Allen, was a super chap so it was easy to get together to plan our trip. With Flg Off Allen and his crew in K-King, I piloted my Horsa glider – BT114 – along with second pilot Sgt Blackburn (he was killed later in a night flying accident shortly before D-Day) and three RAF flyers as witnesses, and we took off from Keevil airfield in Wiltshire on 25 April 1944.

We got up to 14,880ft and Flg Off Allen informed me by intercom along the glider tow rope that he had reached as high as he could with a glider in tow. I asked him to get as much speed up as he could flying straight and level. I pulled off at my chosen time and pulled up into stall position, reaching 15,000ft – a record which still stands today. It took 45 mins to descend to Keevil.

Operation 'Overlord'

Stirlings played a prominent part in the momentous events on the eve of D-Day in Phase II of Operation 'Tonga', when the four squadrons dropped men of the British 6th Airborne Division around the vital bridges over the River Orne and the Caen Canal to secure the left flank of the Allied landings which took place on the following morning – 6 June. In the early evening of D-Day, a 256-strong force of tugs and gliders – sixty-nine of which were Stirlings – took off from seven airfields in southern England on Operation 'Mallard', carrying troops of the 6th Air Landing Brigade and additional divisional troops of the 6th Airborne Division as reinforcements for the 6th Airborne Division holding the left flank of the invasion bridgehead.

Flg Off John Hibbs was a bomb aimer with No 196 Squadron, one of two Stirling squadrons (the other was 299) based at Keevil near Trowbridge in Wiltshire, nestling in lush farmland close to the foot of Salisbury Plain. Although trained as a bomb aimer, John never dropped a live bomb – his task was to drop things like containers, gliders and paratroops. He also doubled up as second pilot, gunner and emergency navigator, although his main occupation in the air was map reading.

John's crew came from all walks of life: his skipper, Brian Arnold, had only recently qualified as an architect before volunteering for aircrew; the navigator, Bill Purser, was a chemist from Nottingham; Ken Nuttall, the wireless op, was a Canadian from Paris, Ontario; Keith Nicholson was the rear gunner and Ginger Hayward the flight engineer.

When the crew came together in December 1943 at Woolfox Lodge in Rutland, both John and Ginger were flight sergeants while the others held commissions. In 1944 John was commissioned but Ginger expressed a desire to remain as an NCO. The crew stayed together throughout a very long and unbroken tour of duty, between December 1943 and June 1945. It only broke up when, in March 1946, the squadron was disbanded after its crews had flown their Stirlings to Northern Ireland for disposal.

In February 1944, No 196 Squadron converted to the Stirling IV at Tarrant Rushton, Dorset, and in April moved to Keevil, from where the squadron took part in the D-Day operations, dropping paratroops near Caen on the night of

5/6 June. But, as John Hibbs recalls, the build-up to D-Day was far from plain sailing and dropping paratroops at night was a difficult task.

> Actually, it all started on 28 May when the aerodrome was sealed off to the public, guards were posted at all the entrances, all leave cancelled and all those on leave were recalled. Then, on the 29th, all the aircrew to be involved – and that included most of our squadron – were taken for briefing.

Bearing their recently applied three white and two black invasion stripes, Stirlings of No 299 Squadron at Keevil are marshalled ready to receive their cargoes of paratroops from the 5th Parachute Brigade for Phase II of Operation 'Tonga', 5 June 1944. *IWM CH21186*

Flg Off John Hibbs (right) flew as a bomb aimer with No 196 Squadron from Keevil on Operation 'Tonga'. He is pictured here with Flg Off Ken Nuttall, wireless op, Flt Lt Brian Arnold, pilot and the ubiquitous bicycles that were to be found on every RAF station. *J. HIBBS*

We were conveyed in coaches with blacked-out windows to an army camp somewhere on Salisbury Plain. Once there we were told in the strictest secrecy that we were to take part the following night in the opening of a second front in Europe.

We were told the details of our particular section of the landings and that there would be other beach-heads created. We were then split up into our various disciplines for more detailed briefing.

At this point we were told precisely when and where we would join a stream of aircraft over England and we were made aware that there would be a number of these streams. The route across the Channel would be marked at fairly frequent intervals by pairs of naval vessels and these would provide rescue facilities should we get into difficulties.

Then we were shown large-scale maps of the dropping zone just northeast of Caen and we were told precisely where the enemy AA batteries were situated. We were informed that just ahead of our flight the naval guns would send down a barrage to eliminate completely the shore batteries and that the Pathfinder Force would obliterate the batteries further inland.

Next we were shown an exact scale model of the coastal dropping zone and invited to imagine a flight over it. Finally we were shown a film taken by Pathfinder Mosquitos of the flight we would be taking the next day. It was the most thorough briefing I ever had. As the world now knows, the next day the weather broke up and the operation was postponed.

At 14.00hrs on 2 June a ban was imposed on the camp, forbidding the exit of any personnel on any pretext, on pain of being shot at sight. Flying was restricted to really necessary air tests while ground crews were heavily involved in painting their Stirlings with the distinctive black and white invasion stripes. 'On 5 June we were called into our briefing room to be told the op was on – a week late. As this was the biggest thing we had done, we were naturally very anxious but also very excited as we realised something of the scale and importance of the operation.'

The scenes around the airfield before take-off were memorable indeed, with forty-six Stirlings from the station's two squadrons lined up in sequence at the end of the runway, while the paratroops of the 13th Battalion, 6th Airborne Division were busily engaged in fitting their parachutes, helped by willing ground crews. Those who were there to witness the final moments before take-off will never forget the tremendous spirit and enthusiasm of these troops who, in the words of one observer, were 'obviously just aching to have a go at the Hun'.

John Hibbs continues:

We took off about dusk and joined a long stream of aircraft over England. Then in the dark we set out for France. Below us in the Channel we could just make out the shapes of pairs of vessels keeping station to mark our route. As we approached the French coast, exactly to the minute we saw the naval guns open up and the resulting explosions as they obliterated the AA batteries, and further inland we could see the flashes as the RAF did the same to the inland batteries.

For most of the trip I sat in the second pilot's seat assisting the pilot, but as we neared the coast I went down to the bombing position. Lying face-down in the nose I was able to recognise the outline of the coast although it was a dark and moonless night. I then took over the direction of the aircraft from the navigator by map reading (part of my duties).

Throughout the journey we had been aware of dark shapes all around us and we knew we were part of a vast body of aircraft. However, as we approached the Dropping Zone (DZ), someone let off a candelabra flare lighting up the whole sky. It was simply full of aircraft. There were aircraft above us, below us and on either side of us. Some ahead of us were beginning to release their paratroops and two in particular that were slightly above us caused two long streams of 'chutes which Brian our pilot had to steer between. Actually, some of the parachutes came very close to our Stirling and afterwards I was told that some aircraft had returned with 'chutes wrapped around their props.

The view looking aft from the astrohatch of Flt Sgt Keith Prowd's No 196 Squadron Stirling IV on 8 June 1944 – D-Day+2. Supply containers are dropped to Allied troops in the vicinity of Ranville and Periers. Other Stirlings can be seen following in the background, dropping their loads. *K. PROWD via K.A. MERRICK*

Plt Off Ray Clements and his crew joined No 620 Squadron from No 1665 HCU in January 1944 and flew right through until the war's end on Stirling IVs. Like many crews in No 38 Group, they flew some of the longest unrelieved tours of duty in the RAF during the Second World War. Since there was no cut-off figure for a tour (Bomber Command Main Force types flew a thirty-op first tour, and twenty for a second tour, although Pathfinder Force tours were sixty ops), crews like Clements' carried on until the war ended or they got the chop, whichever came soonest. They flew on the D-Day drop, Arnhem and the Rhine crossing, and saw the war out to convert to Halifax VIIs in June 1945, flying from Aqir, Palestine.

Standing, left to right: Flt Sgt J.H. Bryce, bomb aimer; Plt Off R.F. Clements, pilot; Flg Off Jack Hilton, navigator; Sgt A. Schofield, flight engineer. Front row: Flt Sgt Percy Hamley, rear gunner; and Plt Off Joe Martin, wireless operator.
R. SEELEY

Nearing our point of release I found that we were flying into a hail of tracer shells. As this was my first time under fire I became tensed up and felt my jaw muscles lock so that I had to make a conscious effort to release them. However, I had to give my attention to the job in hand and having identified the target I pressed the button for the lights telling the paratroopers to jump. The twenty men jumped on time and on target.

This was the first time we had dropped troops at night, and this was the procedure. The troops were lined up on either side of the fuselage, the parachutes on their backs were each attached to static lines (webbing strops), which in turn were connected to little trolleys which ran on steel rails hung from the roof on each side of the fuselage. At the signal – first a red warning light and then a green – the troops jumped into the bath-sized hole in the floor of the rear fuselage. The strops remained attached inside and as each man reached the end of his strop on jumping out, it pulled the release gear from his parachute and the 'chute was released, leaving its outer cover dangling from the strop.

To emphasise the enormous size of the Stirling and its main wheels in particular, Flt Sgt 'Junior' Bryce and Plt Off Joe Martin pose beside one of No 620 Squadron's Mk IVs at Fairford in the summer of 1944, against the backdrop of a busy servicing area. *R. SEELEY*

When all the men had gone it was the duty of the flight engineer, Ginger Hayward, and myself to haul all the straps and casings back on board. This was done by means of two winches attached to the floor on either side at the front of the Stirling. Ginger and I each played out a wire from his winch and taking it down the fuselage, attached it to the bundle of straps on his side and began to wind them in. As they came in the work became harder and harder and eventually in the very dim light of the fuselage we could see a large lump flopping up and down in the well. Both Ginger and I thought with horror that we still had one of our paratroops attached to the straps. Great was our relief when we finally landed the lump to find that all the parachute cases had become entangled together and there was no paratrooper among them.

Three days later we attempted to take supplies to the beach-head but we were recalled part way due to bad weather. Finally, on the 10th, we flew in daylight with a load of twenty-four containers and two special packs and dropped them at the Landing Zone. We had all the excitement of seeing the 'Mulberry' harbour in place and all the furious activity on the ground. One of our special packs was a pair of tractor tyres which we had just tied together and pushed out through the paratroop hatch with no parachute. The rear gunner watched them fall to earth and said they came apart and went bounding in great leaps across the dropping zone hotly pursued by a soldier in a jeep.

One of the 900 or so paratroopers who boarded the Stirlings in the late evening of 5 June at Keevil for the big drop over Normandy was Lt 'Dixie' Dean of the Medium Machine Gun Platoon, the 13th Battalion (Lancashire), the Parachute Regiment, which formed a part of the British 6th Airborne Division.

Stirling IVs of No 196 Squadron line the taxiway at Keevil in the spring of 1944, awaiting take-off.
K. PROWD via K.A. MERRICK

Along with nineteen other members of his platoon Dixie Dean emplaned in Stirling IV LJ819 of No 299 Squadron, nicknamed 'H for Hellzapoppin', piloted by Flt Sgt Jack Gilbert DFM, RAAF. Their destination was Drop Zone 'N', an area covering 2.5sq miles on the east side of the River Orne, just to the north of the village of Ranville and a few miles inland from the Normandy coast. Their task was to take over the defence of the Orne and Caen Canal bridges, captured by glider-borne infantry just after midnight, then clear the enemy and ground obstructions from the Landing Zone north of Ranville so that seventy-two gliders carrying guns, transport and heavy equipment could land at 03.30hrs, some two hours before first light.

'Hellzapoppin', loaded with twenty paratroopers and nine weapons containers, left Keevil's runway at 23.48hrs and headed off into the night.

Lt 'Dixie' Dean of the 6th Airborne Division took part in Phase II of Operation 'Tonga' when he was dropped over DZ 'N' at Ranville in the early hours of 6 June from Stirling LJ819 of No 299 Squadron. *D. DEAN*

Until approximately 00.40hrs on 6 June the flight had been uneventful. True, it was unbearably hot inside the fuselage, but with twenty closely packed bodies all weighted down with 'chutes and 60lb-plus of equipment it was hardly surprising, and the 'in-flight' tea was too sweet for my taste, but the rest of the platoon relished it.

The normal procedure of a '20 minutes to go' signal was received via Sgt 'Cheshire' Kelly, the stick commander who, as No 10 in the jumping order, was plugged into the aircraft's intercom. At the same time back came the wireless operator, Flt Sgt B.A. Croft RAAF, to act as despatcher.

Sgt Kelly gave the order to 'Stand up, hook up,' whereupon we hooked the end of the static line dangling down from the top of our parachute packs to the clip at the end of the strop attached to the roof of the fuselage. Next he ordered 'Check equipment,' followed by 'Sound off for equipment check.' These checks having been carried out, the last man in the stick called out 'No 20 OK,' and so it went on 'No 19 OK' until finally I called 'No 1 OK. Stick OK.' (I found the Stirling was a good aircraft to parachute from, second only to the Dakota.)

My next job should have been to unbolt the forward end of the trap door which covered the aperture through which we were to exit. At the same time the wireless operator would unbolt the rear end, but looking back down the aircraft I could see that he had not yet fixed the strop guard in position. Accordingly, I signalled to No 2, L/Cpl H. Turner, to unhook me and I went back and helped to lower and pin in place the strop guard, rejoined the stick and was hooked up again.

British paratroops on a training exercise familiarise themselves with the hole in the floor through which they will one day jump into battle.
IWM CH21192

Opposite, bottom:
No 196 Squadron's Stirling IV, W-Whisky, lumbers into the air with a Horsa in tow from Keevil on 12 May 1944 on one of the many practice sessions before D-Day.
IWM CH18786

Gliders of the British 6th
Airborne Division on landing
zone 'N' near Ranville, 6 June
1944. *IWM MH2076*

I had still not heard the signal '5 minutes to go', so when we opened the doors and looked down through the aperture I was confused by the fact that we were flying over land. Since the DZ was only a few miles in from the coast, by my reckoning we should have been over the Channel at this stage.

There was another puzzle, too: what were all those white blobs in the dark landscape below? We were flying at 600ft. Surely we were near Dover I thought, and I was looking at chalk spoil thrown up when shells from long-range guns had exploded.

My mind was in a whirl as I looked down when, from behind me, came a positive bellow of 'Green on!' This was the signal to jump, yet I hadn't had the '5 minutes to go' or the 5-second red light of 'Action Stations'.

I hesitated looking first at the 'Green' then at the ground, then at the 'Green' again, and I thought that if I hesitated much longer the lads would think I was going to refuse to jump. So I took that one pace forward and out of the Stirling I went into the cool of the night.

In a way it was a blessing that I had delayed that second or two in making my exit for, having looked around after my 'chute had developed, I decided that those two parallel ribbons of silver shining in the moonlight were the River Orne and the Caen Canal. Further round, the firework display was the ack-ack defences of Caen towards which the aircraft was flying. Looking down I could see I was coming in to land among trees, but by pulling down on my lift webs I was able to steer myself away, although I still managed to land in a tree on the very edge of the DZ. Had I not delayed in jumping, I would have ended up in the middle of an orchard.

By the time we were ready to move out from the rendezvous towards our objective, only eight members of the stick had checked in, although three more joined us later in the day. The rest of the stick from No 12 onwards are STILL missing.

No 11, Ken Lang, was the last man to jump. I landed on the extreme eastern edge of the DZ, Ken just off the western side. Instead of flying north–south down its length, we had flown diagonally across its centre. John Surgey, who jumped No 9, told me that as No 8 – Taffy Price – was about to jump, the red light came on, the signal to stop jumping. But Nos 8, 9, 10 and 11 ignored it.

I assume the bomb aimer, Sgt L.G. Knight – the man who controlled the parachuting – had realised he was running out of DZ and through the light signal suspended the first run-in. What exactly happened after that we will never know for sure.

The remaining nine paratroops never jumped, and 30-year-old Flt Sgt Jack Gilbert and his crew in 'Hellzapoppin' never saw home again. Jack Gilbert had reported over the intercom that there was a lot of flak about and it is quite likely that the aircraft was hit by light flak after aborting its first run-in and crashed in the sea off the French coast. No trace of the aircraft, its crew of six and the nine paratroops has ever been found.

In common with over 20,000 other Allied airmen of the Second World War who have no known grave, the names of Jack Gilbert and his crew are recorded on the Commonwealth Air Forces Memorial at Runnymede in Surrey. The words of Psalm 139, engraved on the glass of the great window of the shrine, are a fitting epitaph to these lost boys:

> If I climb up into Heaven Thou are there.
> If I go down to Hell Thou are there also.
> If I take the wings of the morning and remain
> In the uttermost parts of the sea;
> Even there also shall Thy hand lead me
> and Thy right hand shall hold me.

Operation 'Market Garden'

The morning of Sunday 17 September dawned fine but overcast. Clouds sailed high up in the sky. What little breeze there was barely stirred the grass of the airfields in southern England where a vast airborne armada crouched and waited. Over the next three days, this huge armada would carry over 10,000 men and tow 812 Horsa and 64 Hamilcar gliders to Holland alongside aircraft of the USAAF, in the greatest airborne operation ever mounted.

The plan was to drop paratroops and gliderborne forces along the line Eindhoven-Nijmegen-Arnhem with the primary task of capturing the road

Bright sunlight slants through the haze of an autumn morning to gild the wings of these No 620 Squadron Stirling IVs, standing at Fairford during Operation 'Market Garden' in September 1944. *R. SEELEY*

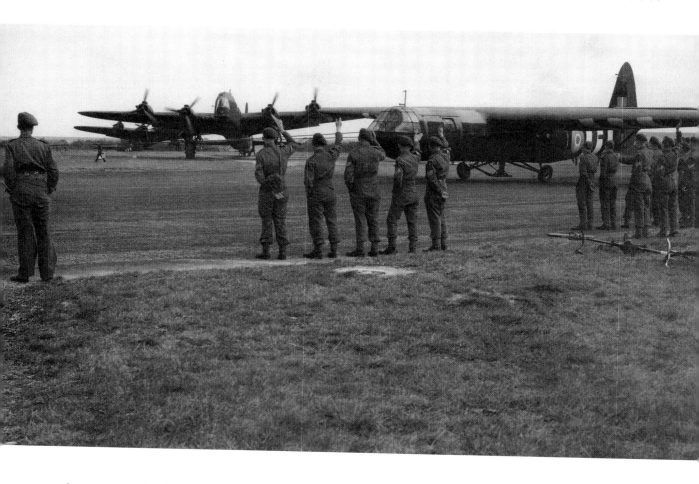

Good Luck: NCOs of the Glider Pilot Regiment (GPR) line the runway's edge to wave off a Horsa on the first 'lift' as it begins its take-off run behind a Stirling at either Keevil or Fairford – destination Arnhem, landing zone 'Z', four miles west of the town. *IWM CH13874*

bridges over the Rivers Maas, Waal and Neder Rijn, and five other waterways. In so doing, a corridor 50 miles long would be cleared for Allied armoured and motorised units to drive north from the Meuse-Escaut Canal to the Zuider Zee. With this daring daylight strike, Montgomery hoped to cut Holland in two, outflank the Siegfried Line and establish the 2nd Army beyond the Rhine on the northernmost edge of the Ruhr, bringing the war in Europe to a close by the end of 1944.

The plan relied heavily on good weather to facilitate the dropping of troops and supplies, combined with a low attrition rate. Because there were insufficient transport aircraft to carry the whole force of three divisions in one 'lift', it was necessary to phase the delivery operation over three days.

Stirlings were very much in the forefront of proceedings to lift a total of 8,969 troops from the British 1st Airborne Division, aided by 1,384 glider pilots, in three lifts. The American effort was performed by C-47s of the USAAF's 50th, 52nd and 53rd Troop Carrier Wings, bearing the US 82nd and 101st Airborne Divisions.

The first sod of earth in 'Market Garden' was cut at 12.40hrs on the 17th when eighty-six Pathfinders of the 21st Independent Parachute Company were dropped from 12 Stirlings of Nos 190 and 620 Squadrons to mark out the landing areas on Zones 'S' and 'X', five miles west of Arnhem, for the airborne troops that were to follow.

In the first lift, gliderborne troops of the 1st Air Landing Brigade were delivered to their landing zone by Stirlings of Nos 190 and 620 Squadrons from Fairford, followed by paratroops of the 1st Parachute Brigade dropped by Stirlings of Nos 196 and 299 Squadrons from Keevil, meeting with very little in the way of enemy resistance. But for the second and third lifts on the 18th and 19th, the storm broke.

Faulty Allied intelligence assessments had underestimated the efficacy of the German 9th and 10th SS Panzer Divisions, refitting a few miles north of Arnhem, and the presence of German Field Marshal Walter Model, Commander of Army Group B. Within 24hrs, Model had ordered his Panzers to mount a powerful counter-attack which brought the advance of the lightly armed Allied airborne troops to a halt. In a story of great valour and numerous instances of personal bravery, the objective of taking the bridge at Arnhem within 48hrs of landing degenerated into a pitched battle in which the airborne troops were forced into a rapidly shrinking pocket, deprived of supplies through a cruel combination of circumstances. Allied aircraft on resupply operations were forced to fly low through curtains of withering ground fire and run the gauntlet of enemy fighters in broad daylight in order to get the badly needed supplies through.

John Hibbs and his No 196 Squadron crew flew on both the first and third lifts:

> Our trip to Arnhem was another well-planned daylight operation that went disastrously wrong. On this occasion we were towing Horsa gliders full of troops of the 1st Airborne LT Regiment RA. The first day our route took us across the North Sea and, like D-Day, was again marked by pairs of naval vessels at intervals. The route was northeast to the Dutch islands and then up the Waal river to Arnhem.
>
> The whole trip was calm with little opposition and we dropped the glider over the target on time. Two days later we went again with another glider, but this time our route was further south through Belgium then Eindhoven and up the Nijmegen corridor to Arnhem. The corridor was a narrow strip of land held by the Allies with the Germans encamped on either side, with the result that we were shot at by light AA fire for most of the way.
>
> As the first trip had been so peaceful we had with us the adjutant of 'D' Squadron of the Glider Pilot Regiment who had come along for the ride. He was just taking a turn at piloting the Stirling when the flak started. He commented on the 'fluffy little clouds' which had started

En Route: Stirlings of No 620 Squadron head towards Arnhem by way of Hatfield, Aldeburgh and West Schouwen on 17 September, at a height of 2,500ft. In tow are Horsa gliders of 'D' Squadron, GPR, carrying troops and equipment of the 1st Air Landing Brigade. The aircraft from which this photograph was taken, Stirling IV LK127 QS:O, flew just three ops with the squadron before it was lost on a resupply drop to Arnhem on 20 September, coming down at Heteren on the southern side of the Rhine in full view of the beleaguered troops of the 1st Airborne Division. *N. CHAFFEY*

The pilot of No 295 Squadron's Stirling IV 'Shorty George' pokes his head out of the cockpit window to make a final visual check on his engineless charge. With a hiss like startled cobras, the brakes are released as a batman on the runway beckons the Stirling slowly forward to take up the slack on the tow rope hooked to the Horsa. With a green light from the control van away to the left of the runway, 'Shorty George's' 'taps' are opened and, with a tremendous surge of latent power, the combination of Stirling and Horsa moves off down the runway at Harwell carrying men of the 1st Airborne Division to Arnhem. *IWM CH13875*

Above: Stirling IV, LJ977 'Beer is Best', of No 570 Squadron, heading for Arnhem. *T. WOOD via JR/SBRL*

Sketch to show the procedure for take-off used by tugs and gliders in 1944–5. Stirling tugs line the runway margins, each one hooked up to a Horsa glider positioned on the runway. *B.A. STAIT*

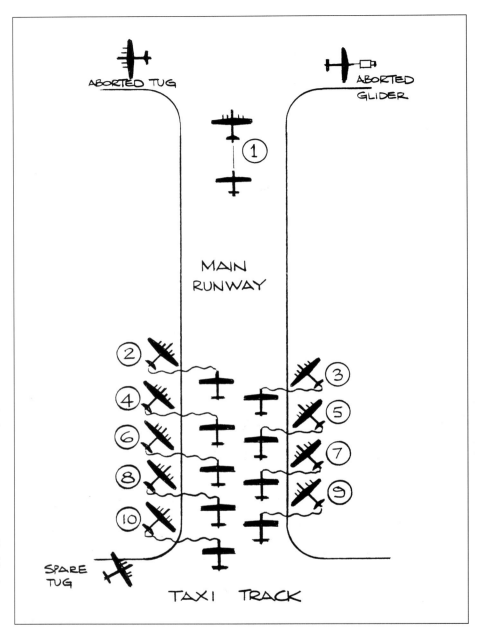

Opposite: Piloted by Capt Hugh Bartlett, a Horsa of 'A' Squadron, GPR is towed through broken cloud at 2,500ft and about 140kt en route to Arnhem, some 350ft behind Stirling IV LJ977 'Beer is Best' (see previous page, top right) of No 570 Squadron, skippered by the squadron's CO, Wg Cdr R.J. Bangay.

Both Bangay and Bartlett completed the three big airborne ops of the war – 'Overlord', 'Market Garden' and 'Varsity' – and on each occasion flew together in the same glider and tug combination.

Of the 359 tugs and gliders which flew to Arnhem on the first lift on 17 September, thirty-nine gliders failed to reach their LZs through a combination of broken tow-ropes and tugs with engine

appearing, but on being told they were flak bursts he dropped his hands from the control column in horror.

We released our glider over the target correctly and made two subsequent trips to Arnhem with supplies which we dropped on target, despite being shot at for most of the way. However, on our return home we learned with horror that our supplies had been reaching the enemy who had taken the dropping zones. On one of these resupply drops we brought our Stirling back with seven of its fourteen petrol tanks holed,

including one of those in the wing roots that were not self-sealing. After we had landed back at Keevil, taxied in to dispersal and switched off, we could hear the sound of a tap running which, in fact, was petrol pouring out of the wing.

Sqn Ldr James Stewart, 'B' Flight Commander with No 570 Squadron at the time of 'Market Garden', witnessed the loss of one of his Stirling crews to flak:

On one of the resupply sorties following the Arnhem battle, one of the crews in my flight was flying in formation with me and was hit just after crossing the Rhine. All four engines were on fire so he turned away and recrossed the river, finishing in a ball of fire which I witnessed. Naturally,

Opposite, top: Fairford: air and ground crews enjoy an alfresco brew-up in between resupply drops during Operation 'Market Garden'. *R. SEELEY*

Opposite, bottom: Harwell: Flt Lts Scott and Walters (centre) of No 570 Squadron are pictured on the second day of the ill-fated Arnhem drop when the squadron towed 10 Horsas to LZ 'X' to the west of Arnhem with the second lift of the 1st Air Landing Brigade. *T. WOOD via JR/SBRL*

Above: Homeward Bound: By mid-afternoon on 17 September, most of the tugs and their crews were safely home, but for the troops of the 1st Airborne Division it was only the beginning of a hard-fought battle which would end in either death or imprisonment. Stirling IV LK171 'Shooting Stars' is pictured returning from Arnhem after the first lift, skippered by 32-year-old Grp Capt Wilfred Surplice DSO, DFC, station commander at Rivenhall, Essex. Because LK171 was placed at the personal disposal of Surplice it did not carry the regular squadron codes of either of the Rivenhall squadrons, instead bearing his personal initials: WES. These it wore until the day it crashed in bad weather on a supply drop to Norwegian Resistance forces on 2/3 November 1944. Surplice ordered his crew to bale out after the Stirling iced up and became difficult to handle. All of the crew managed to escape from the doomed aircraft before it crashed into a mountain near Rjukan at Skarfjell, killing Surplice. *R. DALTON via JR/SBRL*

I assumed that all the crew had been killed and on my return wrote the usual letters to the next-of-kin.

The following morning I received a telephone call from the captain of that aircraft with the request that I send someone to pick him and all his crew up from Brussels where they had spent a hectic night having hitched a lift in a truck belonging to the Guards' Armoured Brigade who were passing down the road from Nijmegen.

The pilot had managed to guide the aircraft between two brick-making kilns which tore the wings off, leaving the fuselage to fly on 50 or so yards before coming to rest and allowing the crew to escape. The ball of fire I had seen from the air was the moment at which the two wings, plus fuel, had parted company from the fuselage.

Montgomery, realising the impossibility of the situation, ordered the withdrawal of his troops south of the river under cover of darkness on 25/26 September, although the losses sustained by the 1st Airborne Division were heavy: some 6,200 taken prisoner and 1,500 killed, for over 3,000 of the enemy killed. But the bridge remained untaken.

The Stirling element which supported the operation also paid a high price in losses of crews and aircraft. Low-level daylight drops of gliders and supplies from heights of 2,000ft and even lower meant the aircraft were very vulnerable to light flak and small arms fire, not to mention German fighters. Due to communications problems experienced by the British troops on the ground, the valiant efforts of RAF Stirling and Dakota crews to drop much-needed supplies were to little avail, with the most part falling into enemy hands after Allied ground positions had been overrun.

Stirling losses to enemy fighters and flak during the resupply operations amounted to sixty-three aircraft shot down and badly damaged – a significant proportion of No 38 Group's Stirling force.

Operation
'Varsity'

With the bitter lessons of Arnhem fresh in their minds, the Allied Planning Staff's scheme for Operation 'Varsity' – the airborne assault on the River Rhine – was another massive operation, but this time a far simpler affair in its organisation. Ground assault troops of the US 9th and British 2nd Armies would cross the Rhine west of the German town of Wesel on 24 March 1945 after the enemy positions on the opposite bank had been pulverised by heavy bombing raids and a withering artillery barrage.

Two airborne divisions were then to be dropped, their tasks to take and hold the Diesfordter Forest on the high ground northwest of Wesel, secure local bridges over the River Issel and then link up with the Allied ground forces advancing across the Rhine.

The key to success lay in the resupply of the airborne troops some 6hrs after their landing, and not at a later date as at Arnhem.

As part of an overall plan involving the US 17th Airborne Division to land 21,680 Allied troops in a single airlift by parachute and glider, the British effort involved 440 tugs and gliders, of which 200 were supplied by the six Stirling squadrons, carrying troops of the British 6th Airborne Division.

On 24 March at airfields in southern England, dawn had barely broken before the brittle tranquility of the spring morning was shattered by over 1,500 aeroengines bursting into life, heralding the biggest tactical air assault ever mounted on Hitler's 'Festung Europa'. Forming up over Essex, the paratroop Dakotas of No 46 Group took 18 minutes to pass overhead, followed by the Stirling, Halifax and Dakota glider combinations of Nos 38 and 46 Groups in a 39-minute stream. Crossing the French coast at Cap Gris Nez, the RAF formation rendezvoused with the USAAF contingent south of Brussels to form a

Above: '555 State Express' was the personal mount of Sqn Ldr James Stewart, 'B'
Flight commander on No 570 Squadron at Rivenhall. 'My aircraft was serialled LK555
so, not unnaturally, my ground crew nicknamed it 'State Express' after the well-known
brand of cigarettes.

'The glider pilot who trained behind me was one S/Sgt Sullivan. When the day
dawned in March 1945 for take-off on "Varsity", he was sitting behind me in Horsa
glider "333", strangely another brand of State Express cigarette.

'The drill was that if the tow rope broke on take-off, the tug aircraft went to the
end of the taxi rank and the next aircraft took over the glider thus left. Because of the
relationship between "555" and "333", neither Sullivan nor I was going to let the
coincidence be broken when our tow rope snapped.

'So, the war was halted for a couple of minutes while I taxied round at the end of
the runway and hastily returned to take up another rope with "333" at the other end.
Happily, we got airborne without further mishap and "333" finally landed in Germany
near the town of Wesel.' *J. STEWART*

Opposite, top: Stirlings of No 620
Squadron line up at Great Dunmow
ready for Operation 'Varsity' on
24 March 1945. Horsa gliders can be
seen lined up on the left of the picture;
a towing cable lies in the foreground.
A number of Halifax tugs are also visible
in the background. *N. CHAFFEY*

Opposite, bottom: No 295
Squadron at Rivenhall despatched thirty
Stirlings and Horsas for 'Varsity', losing
one aircraft to flak.

Pictured here standing in front of
their 'B' Flight Stirling IV at Rivenhall are
Ken Longman, Syd Hoskins, 'Casey'
Jones (skipper), 'Micky' Finn, Frank
Danton and Ken Morris.

MRS K. DANTON via JR/SBRL

In this movie still of the take-offs from Rivenhall for Operation 'Varsity', No 570 Squadron's Stirling IV LK555 '555 State Express' takes to the air with Sqn Ldr James Stewart at the controls, towing Horsa '333' (off the edge of the picture). *J. STEWART*

vast armada of 2,931 aircraft and gliders that headed east towards Wesel. The first paratroops were scheduled to jump at 10.00hrs and the first British gliders to land at 10.21hrs.

No 620 Squadron's diarist recorded the conditions prevailing on the day of the Rhine crossing:

> Weather over the whole route was magnificent, no better conditions could have prevailed. There was no opposition en route although small numbers of light AA guns offered ineffective opposition near to the landing zones. A smoke pall, caused by the previous artillery barrage laid down, hung over the landing zones, but visibility was good enough to pick out individual landing zones without difficulty.

By 14.30hrs, success for the Allies was in sight and, by 15.00hrs that same day, German resistance crumbled as the advancing ground armies linked up with their airborne compatriots. The fate of Nazism had been sealed.

A New Shape
in the Skies

The ultimate version of the basic Stirling design was the long-nosed Mk V, conceived by Shorts during 1943 as its Plan 'C' for a civil freight/passenger variant to compete on the postwar airliner market.

In common with the Mk IV, nose and mid-upper turrets were deleted, but the Mk V design went further with the deletion of the rear turret and the addition of an upward-hinging nose section forward of the cockpit. A large downward-hinging cargo door measuring 9ft 6in by 5ft 1in, fitted in the starboard rear fuselage side, facilitated the loading of bulky items such as Jeeps.

Powered by four 1,635hp Bristol Hercules XVI air-cooled radials, the first two production Mk Vs, out of a total of 160, were delivered to the RAF at No 23 MU, Aldergrove, on 16 September 1944. They were painted in a distinctive

Displaying the new colour scheme, this unidentified Stirling V is pictured on an air test in late 1945. Also of note are the propeller spinners, occasionally used in conjunction with cooling fans fitted under the cowlings of Mk IVs and Vs to help prevent engines from overheating.
IWM MH6858

scheme of dark green/medium grey/azure blue, that contrasted sharply with the drab Bomber Command scheme of dark green/dark earth/night black. After the war, many Mk Vs were stripped down to a bare metal finish which gave the aircraft a marginal increase in cruising speed.

Various load configurations were possible with the Stirling V, including mixed freight and passenger loads with seating for a maximum of forty passengers. Alternatively, twenty fully-equipped paratroops could be carried or, in the casualty evacuation role, twelve stretchers or fourteen sitting cases could be accommodated.

The first RAF squadrons to equip with the new mark were Nos 46 and 242, their first training flights to foreign climes being made in February 1945. By the end of April, No 46 Squadron was operating regular scheduled freight and passenger flights to India. Two more UK-based squadrons, Nos 51 and 158, were equipped with the mark at the end of the war, together with two Heavy Freight Flights which operated five Stirling Vs each between the Middle East and India (No 1588), and the UK and the Middle East (No 1589). No 196 Squadron had a brief encounter with the mark during early 1946, but it was No 1588 Flight that became the last RAF unit to operate the Stirling, finally retiring its Mk Vs in July 1946 after the more capable Avro York had assumed the mantle of long-range transport for the RAF.

But the Stirling story was not quite over, the final chapter being written with the purchase of at least ten converted Mk Vs by the Belgian carrier Trans-Air of Melsbroek in 1947. The aircraft were used on freight and passenger charter operations between Europe and China by Trans-Air and Air Transport, also based at Melsbroek. However, their careers were short and all were withdrawn from service in 1948, although up to six were sold to Egypt in 1948/49.

An interior view of the Stirling's somewhat spartan passenger cabin, looking forward to the rear wing spar where extra windows have been fitted above the wing roots. On the right can be seen part of the fuselage cargo door which extends aft some 9ft. For passengers travelling on the epic twelve-day flight from the UK to India, operated thrice-weekly from October 1945, the journey must have seemed like an endurance exercise with little in the way of creature comforts.

IWM CH16483

No 196 Squadron had a two-month dalliance with the Stirling V before it disbanded at the end of March 1946. These two photographs taken during February/March 1946 show Mk V PK144 in natural metal finish, 'lobbing in' at Rivenhall, Essex, and later at rest on its dispersal. *VIA B.A. STAIT*

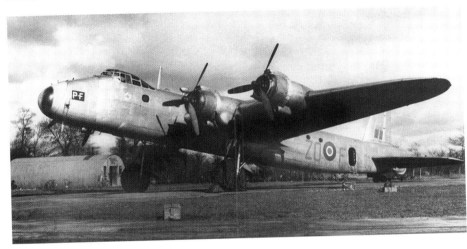

Below: The huge bulk of a Stirling V looms over this group of No 196 Squadron aircrew, pictured at Rivenhall in early 1946. *J. HIBBS*

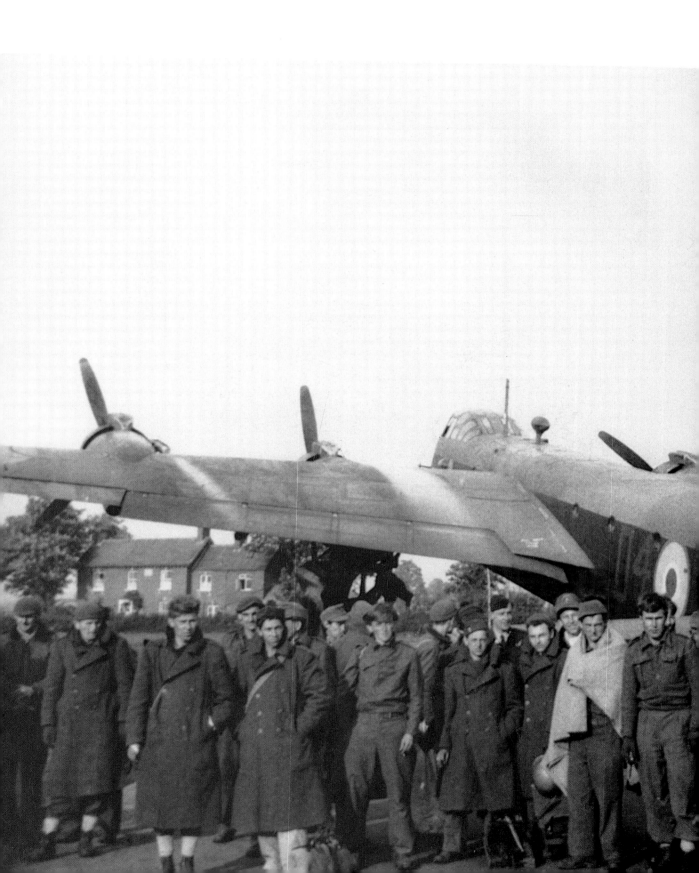

Home from the war: these American former PoWs experience their first heady taste of freedom as they pose for the camera on 22 April 1945, after their arrival in the UK at Westcott, Buckinghamshire. Many are wearing 'liberated' German forage caps.

Plt Off Derek de Rome of No 620 Squadron flew all thirty of them home to England in Stirling IV LJ566 'Yorkshire Rose II', after their release from captivity.

'Yorkshire Rose II's' flight engineer, Flt Sgt Frank Pearman, and navigator, Plt Off Ben Crocker, can be seen on the extreme right of the group enjoying a cigarette with a grateful GI. WO Noel Chaffey, wireless operator, who took the photographs, stands beneath the wing trailing edge at centre back.

N. CHAFFEY

Above: Flg Off 'Chuck' Hoysted RAAF of No 196 Squadron poses with his crew and three groundcrew (who had come along for the ride) at Stavanger, Norway, on 18 May 1945, after they had ferried across eighteen troops and supplies from Shepherd's Grove. The aircraft is No 196 Squadron's Mk IV, LK205, D-Dog. *J. PARKER*

Opposite, top: Men of the British 1st Airborne Division wait to join their aircraft at Great Dunmow on 11 May 1945 for Operation 'Doomsday', the airlifting by the squadrons of No 38 Group of Allied troops for the occupation of Norway. *N. CHAFFEY*

Opposite, bottom: Panoply of Power: forty-one Stirlings of Nos 295 and 570 Squadrons line up along the perimeter track and the NW/SE runway at Rivenhall on 11 May 1945 for Operation 'Doomsday'. A further six Stirlings can be seen on dispersals, together with some twenty-four Horsas dotted around the airfield. *P. BALDOCK via B.A. STAIT*

Next spread: Prague – Summer 1945: the rear entrance door of this No 570 Squadron Stirling IV marks the gateway to a brighter future for these Czechoslovak orphans, many of whom were internees in Nazi concentration camps. *IWM CH15898*

Postscript

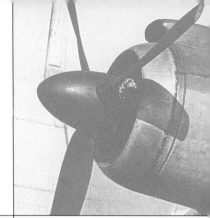

If the Stirling's efforts during the heat of battle were eclipsed by the exploits of its contemporaries the Lancaster and Halifax, Shorts' big bomber suddenly achieved parity when the RAF found itself with huge quantities of surplus aircraft on its hands after the war had ended. Stirling, Lancaster and Halifax finally met on equal terms for the first and last time when each suffered the same ignominious fate at MUs across the country, falling to the scrapman's blowtorch.

In May 1945, WO L.J. Brock, a flight engineer with No 190 Squadron, assisted a Flt Sgt Tucker to fly his old mount on its final trip to the breaker's yard at Maghaberry in Northern Ireland:

> The aircraft [Mk IV LJ824] had been completely stripped of radio and anything removable and we were given 100gals of petrol in each of the main fuel tanks for the one-way trip. We had bad weather over the Irish Sea and had to return to England, but due to the petrol situation we had to land at the first drome we saw, Calveley in Cheshire, with Tiger Moths taking off around us. The following day we took off again and made it to Maghaberry, returning by Dakota.

Flt Lt James McIlhinney, formerly a Stirling navigator with No 218 Squadron, flew to Maghaberry in August 1945 to pick up navigational compasses and other paraphernalia with which to equip a navigational demonstration room at No 7 Air Navigation School, Bishop's Court, Co Down.

For several years, Maghaberry had been an Aircraft Storage Unit under the administration of No 23 MU at Aldergrove, where several hundred Stirlings had

No 46 Squadron was one of the first two RAF units to operate the
Stirling V. In this view of one of the squadron's Mk Vs at Stoney Cross in
1945, the size of the main wheels can be appreciated. *G. MACKIE*

been stored. With the war's end, they were all scrapped. He was astonished to learn that newly completed Stirlings from Shorts in Belfast were being flown the 15 or so miles to Maghaberry, only to be broken up. He also found it hard to discover one single intact compass – workmen had broken them open to get at the alcohol inside (or so the story went).

Neither was operating from bases overseas necessarily a guarantee of longevity for the Stirling, as Cpl J. Hardman, an engineer fitter, recalls:

> My oppo on No 214 Squadron during the Stirling days had been posted to India in 1945 where his task was to help assemble Stirlings delivered in crates. Although they had seventeen serviceable aircraft there were no aircrews to fly them – so they never flew. For over 12 months they were taxied around the airfield by the lads for something to do, always fully fuelled and ready for the off. Before he left, my oppo and the others put them all in the middle of the airfield and set fire to them.

As if to emphasise the Air Ministry's line that the Short Stirling was a complete and utter failure as a bomber aircraft, officialdom did a remarkably neat job in expunging all traces of it by the end of the 1940s. Not one complete aircraft survived out of the 2,383 built.

But the twenty-first century could well see a rebuilt Stirling rise phoenix-like from the ashes. In 1997, The Stirling Project was constituted under the chairmanship of former XV Squadron navigator, Brian Harris, with the immediate aim of preserving components and documentary evidence of this historic aircraft. The committee set itself the long term aim of constructing a forward section of fuselage to production standards, and has embarked on the laborious programme of re-creating the necessary plan drawings. A workshop has been established and conservation of recovered and donated Stirling components is underway. RAF Wyton has donated a hangar for the storage of Stirling aircraft parts, prior to the attempted rebuild. Further information can be found at www.stirlingproject.co.uk

Bibliography

PRIMARY SOURCE MATERIAL
The National Archives (Public Record Office), Kew, Surrey

AIR 14/1442–3: Bomber Command Operational Research Section, 'K' Reports on
   aircraft losses, October 1942–July 1945.

AIR 14/1697: Stirling aircraft bombing installations, March 1941-March 1943.

AIR 25/588: No 38 (Airborne Forces) Group, Appendices, September 1943–June
   1944.

AIR 27/647: No 75 (NZ) Squadron Operations Record Book (ORB).

AIR 27/956: No 138 (SD) Squadron ORB.

AIR 27/1068: No 161 (SD) Squadron ORB.

AIR 27/1154: No 190 Squadron ORB.

AIR 27/1167: No 196 Squadron ORB.

AIR 27/1172: No 199 Squadron ORB.

AIR 27/1352: No 218 Squadron ORB.

AIR 27/1644: No 295 Squadron ORB.

AIR 27/1654: No 299 Squadron ORB.

AIR 27/2041: No 570 Squadron ORB.

AIR 27/2134: No 620 Squadron ORB.

AIR 50/192: Bomber Command Combat Reports.

AVIA 15/3766: Negotiations for use of Austin factory for Stirling production, 1938–39.

AVIA 18/702: Stirling performance and handling trials, 1940–46.

AVIA 18/1277: Longitudinal stability of Stirling aircraft, 1944.

AVIA 18/1374: Report from A&AEE Martlesham Heath, Stirling half-scale aircraft
   handling trials, 24 November 1938.

PUBLISHED SECONDARY SOURCE MATERIAL

Bowyer, C., *For Valour: The Air VCs*, William Kimber, 1978

—, *Bomber Barons*, William Kimber, 1985

—, *Tales from the Bombers*, William Kimber, 1985

Bowyer, M.J.F., *The Stirling Bomber*, Faber, 1980

Crown Copyright, *Pilot's and Flight Engineer's Notes: Stirling I, III, IV*, 1944

Foot, M.R.D., *SOE*, Mandarin, 1990

Gomersall, B., *The Stirling File*, Air Britain, 1979

Jones, W.E., *Bomber Intelligence*, Midland Counties, 1983

Langdon, D., *Punch with Wings*, Arthur Barker Ltd, 1960

Lerche, H-W., *Luftwaffe Test Pilot*, Janes, 1980

McBean, Wg Cdr J.A., and Hogben, Maj A.S., *Bombs Gone*, Patrick Stephens Ltd, 1990

McCall, G., *Flight Most Secret*, William Kimber, 1981

Mackay, R., *Short Stirling in Action*, Squadron/Signal Publications, 1989

Mahaddie, Gp Capt T.G., *Hamish*, Ian Allen, 1989

Marshall, B., *The White Rabbit*, Pan, 1954

Merrick, K.A., *Flights of the Forgotten*, Arms & Armour Press, 1989

Middlebrook, M., *The Berlin Raids*, Viking Penguin, 1988

—, and Everitt, C., *The Bomber Command War Diaries*, Penguin, 1985

Musgrove, G., *Operation Gomorrah*, Janes, 1981

Peden, M., *A Thousand Shall Fall*, Stoddard, 1979

Richards, D., and Saunders, H. StG., *Royal Air Force 1939–1945*, HMSO, 1953

Smith, D.J., *Britain's Military Airfields 1939–45*, Patrick Stephens Ltd, 1989

Stait, B.A., *Rivenhall: The History of an Essex Airfield*, 1984

Storrs, Sir R., *Dunlop in War and Peace*, Hutchinson, 1946

Streetly, M., *Confound and Destroy*, Janes, 1978

Various authors and volumes, *Action Stations*, Patrick Stephens Ltd

Webster, Sir C., and Frankland, N., *The Strategic Air Offensive against Germany 1939-1945*, 4 vols, HMSO, 1961

Wilmot, C., *The Struggle for Europe*, Collins, 1952

Winfield, Dr R., *The Sky Belongs to Them*, William Kimber, 1976

Wood, A., *History of the World's Glider Forces*, Patrick Stephens Ltd, 1990

MAGAZINES AND PERIODICALS

Flight, The Aeroplane, Aeroplane Monthly, Aircraft Illustrated, Aviation News, Airfix Magazine, After the Battle.

In the tropical heat of India, a No 51 Squadron Mk V, PK124:Q, is manhandled along the taxiway at an unidentified airfield during 1946. Visible in this picture are the faired-over tail turret, the outline of the fuselage cargo door and the streamlined hinged nose section with its clear perspex cap. The modifications to the nose and tail added an extra 3ft to the Stirling's overall length. *IWM CI1703*

Index